PRAISE FOR *CONFIDENT LEADER!*

"*Confident Leader!* is the field guide all leaders wish they had years ago! Dan Reiland knows at some point every leader struggles with confidence—whether battling self-sufficiency and control or confronting doubts and insecurity. Filled with memorable personal examples as well as timeless wisdom from God's Word, and with Jesus as the ultimate source, this book is guaranteed to improve the way you lead."

—Chris Hodges, Senior Pastor, Church of the Highlands;
author, *The Daniel Dilemma* and *What's Next?*

"*Confident Leader!* is one of the most important leadership resources to be released in a long time. Dan is a proven and seasoned leader who drops pure leadership gold on every page. He brilliantly shares why confidence is so important and lays out a clear plan to grow in confidence and bounce back from setbacks. Read this and digest it and become the leader you were meant to be."

—Jud Wilhite, Senior Pastor, Central Church; author, *Uncaged*

"Finding the right balance of confidence is tricky, but so essential in today's cultural climate. My friend Dan Reiland cracks the code with honest and insightful help that you can apply to your leadership *today*. It's a practical guide to building the authentic foundation every leader needs. Whatever leadership level you find yourself at, don't miss reading *Confident Leader!*"

—Sherry Surratt, Executive Director of Leadership Strategy, The Rethink Group

"So many leaders struggle with confidence. It's one thing to know you have a problem. It's another to know how to solve it. With humility, wisdom and profound insight, Dan Reiland shows us how to build the kind of confidence you cannot just build your leadership on, but your life on. I'm so grateful for Dan and for this book."

—Carey Nieuwhof, author; Founding Pastor, Connexus Church

"Read this book, and take the principles seriously. Don't skim the pages. Dig in and take a deeper look. *Confident Leader!* will make a difference in your life."

—Dr. John C. Maxwell, bestselling author; speaker; leadership
coach; founder, The John Maxwell Company and EQUIP

"Every leader I coach struggles with confidence. Sometimes we have too much, sometimes not enough—but we all long for more of that authentic and God-focused confidence in which people are helped, God is glorified, and we feel fulfilled. In *Confident Leader!*, Dan masterfully explains the unique dimensions and practical steps we can all take to build our confidence and infuse that confidence into those we lead. Every leader needs this book!"

—Kadi Cole, leadership consultant; executive coach; author, *Developing Female Leaders* (www.kadicole.com)

"Dan Reiland has given us a treasure and road map that shows the way to a leadership that is anchored in a resilient God-confidence. The use of interviews, stories, and illustrations not only compellingly underscores the habits and characteristics of enduring leadership but also motivates us to be pictures of the destination at which we want others to arrive. Thank you, Dan, for this wonderful gift and labor of love!"

—Dr. Crawford W. Loritts, Jr., Senior Pastor, Fellowship Bible Church, Roswell, Georgia; radio host; author, *Unshaken* and *Leadership as an Identity*

"If there was ever a time when leaders needed confidence more than today, I'd have a hard time saying when. Through the pages of *Confident Leader!*, Dan Reiland will help take you there."

—John Ortberg, Senior Pastor, Menlo Church; author, *Eternity Is Now in Session*

"I can't think of a better leader to write this book! Dan Reiland is one of those rare leaders who exudes the type of confidence that leaders are often grappling for. *Confident Leader!* will give you practical instruction for your leadership development supported by personal stories of other confident leaders. This is your guide to keep growing and thriving as a leader!"

—Jenni Catron, author; speaker; founder, The 4Sight Group

"Confidence! I've struggled with it all my life. I've learned to understand and manage it, but now that I've read *Confident Leader!* by my friend Dan Reiland, it all comes together. Thanks Dan for writing with transparency and courage. This book has helped me and will do the same for you."

—Sam Chand, leadership consultant; author, *New Thinking—New Future* (www.samchand.com)

"When Dan asked me to write an endorsement for his new book, I quickly agreed. I believe in Dan's leadership as much as any leader I know. What I didn't realize was how timely the book would be for me! I received Dan's book in a time in my career where I once again need confidence to lead effectively. This book helped me in my current season and I know it will be a blessing for many other leaders."

—Ron Edmondson, CEO, Leadership Network; pastor; church
leadership consultant; author, *The Mythical Leader*

"I recently heard a well-respected leader say, 'If I could wave a magic wand and give every leader one gift, it would be the gift of confidence.' The truth is, it's a gift most of us could use more of. Unfortunately, there isn't a magic wand. But if you want more confidence, Dan's book will walk you through how to get it and it just might be exactly what you need."

—Ashley Wooldridge, Senior Pastor, Christ's Church
of the Valley, Phoenix, Arizona

"You are selecting an excellent leadership resource to read. We have known Dan for several years and always found his insights to be rich and relevant. His transparent writings give us the sense that he understands challenges each of us face. His years of experience in leading successful organizations have taught him how to teach us. Clearly there is an unwavering commitment to add value throughout this book as only a thoughtful mentor can."

—Dennis and Colleen Rouse, Senior Pastors, Victory Church,
Norcross, Georgia; Dennis: author, *10 Qualities That Move You
from a Believer to a Disciple*; Colleen: author; founder, Thrive
Today, Resources for Professional Women of Faith

"Dan Reiland, a leader of leaders, knows what we need to navigate leadership waters. He has given us yet another superb tool for our leadership toolboxes. He shows us a clear road map in three fundamental areas: leadership foundations, character development, and practical disciplines. He unpacks fifteen essentials that help build authentic leadership confidence, a key to healthy success. Every leader should read this book and get a copy for the leaders around them."

—Dr. Charles Stone, Pastor, WestPark Church, London, Ontario; author
of six books, including, *Every Pastor's First 180 Days: How to Start
and Stay Strong in a New Church Job* (www.charlesstone.com)

"The Scriptures remind us that we should 'not think more highly of ourselves than we ought.' But of equal importance is that we 'not think more lowly of ourselves than we ought.' Balancing humility and confidence may be one of the trickiest tightropes a leader can try to walk. Dan Reiland has done a masterful job of outlining how to balance the two. *Confident Leader!* will help your leadership go to the next level!"

—**William Vanderbloemen, CEO and founder, Vanderbloemen Search Group; speaker; author, *Culture Wins***

"Some people are gifted to lead. Others have both the gift and a leadership role. Far fewer, though, leverage their gift, embrace their role, *and* lead with authentic confidence. It's this leadership confidence that tends to set great leaders apart and allows them to leverage their wiring and role for something significant. Dan's book gives us the insights and practical next steps leaders need to lead with confidence."

—**Tony Morgan, founder and Lead Strategist of The Unstuck Group; author, *The Unstuck Church***

"After serving as CEO to John Maxwell for ten years, I can wholeheartedly say that what Dan says in this book is spot on. Developing your confidence as a leader is a process, and his advice for the journey is some of the most powerful I've ever read. You will learn and be better because of this book!"

—**Mark Cole, CEO, The John Maxwell Enterprise**

"*Confident Leader!* is a fresh wind speaking to the depth of what it means to lead . . . NOT prescriptive with a few behaviors and one arrives as a leader . . . NOT developing a cookie-cutter-type leader. BUT, leaders of various styles, circumstances, cultures, gifts, along with biblical and contemporary models that have eternal significance. *Confident Leader!* brings a new message and hope no matter one's age or experience. It is a masterpiece, compelling, and a MUST-READ."

—**Jo Anne Lyon, ambassador, General Superintendent Emerita, The Wesleyan Church**

"One of the most important qualities in leadership is confidence. Confidence energizes a leader and their vision, yet so many leaders struggle with a lack of confidence. In *Confident Leader!* Dan Reiland provides invaluable insight on understanding where true confidence is found and how every leader can lead with authentic courage and certainty."

—**Todd Mullins, Senior Pastor, Christ Fellowship Church, West Palm Beach, Florida**

"I wish I'd read this book in my initial years as a leader! Yet after forty years of leading, Dan speaks into my life in transformative ways—and will yours as well. He deeply and practically unfolds an authentic confidence that avoids arrogance, to 'be strong and courageous' in the unavoidable uncertainty of kingdom risks without the debilitating impact of insecurity."

—Dr. Wayne Schmidt, General Superintendent, The Wesleyan Church

"As you read and engage, you will quickly come to realize that this is not just another book answering a plethora of questions that leaders do not seem to be asking today. I am convinced that *Confident Leader!* will be a close companion to you on your leadership journey toward authentic confidence. Dan's ability to weave together foundational leadership concerns, leadership principles, and practical outworking thereof is to be commended."

—Ed Stetzer, Wheaton College

CONFIDENT LEADER!

BECOME ONE

STAY ONE

DAN REILAND

THOMAS NELSON
Since 1798

Published in Nashville, Tennessee, by Thomas Nelson Books. Thomas Nelson is a registered trademark of HarperCollins Christian Publishing, Inc.

Thomas Nelson titles may be purchased in bulk for educational, business, fund-raising, or sales promotional use. For information, please e-mail SpecialMarkets@ThomasNelson.com.

Scripture quotations are taken from the Holy Bible, New International Version®, NIV®. Copyright © 1973, 1978, 1984, 2011 by Biblica, Inc.® Used by permission of Zondervan. All rights reserved worldwide. www.Zondervan.com. The "NIV" and "New International Version" are trademarks registered in the United States Patent and Trademark Office by Biblica, Inc.®

Scripture quotations marked NASB are from New American Standard Bible®. Copyright © 1960, 1962, 1963, 1968, 1971, 1972, 1973, 1975, 1977, 1995 by The Lockman Foundation. Used by permission. (www.Lockman.org)

Scripture quotations marked NKJV are from the New King James Version®. © 1982 by Thomas Nelson. Used by permission. All rights reserved.

Any Internet addresses, phone numbers, or company or product information printed in this book are offered as a resource and are not intended in any way to be or to imply an endorsement by Thomas Nelson, nor does Thomas Nelson vouch for the existence, content, or services of these sites, phone numbers, companies, or products beyond the life of this book.

ISBN 978-1-4002-1723-6 (eBook)
ISBN 978-1-4002-1720-5 (HC)

Library of Congress Control Number: 2020930811

Printed in the United States of America
20 21 22 23 24   LSC   10 9 8 7 6 5 4 3 2 1

About Leadership ✳ Network

Leadership Network fosters innovation movements that activate the church to greater impact. We help shape the conversations and practices of pacesetter churches in North America and around the world. The Leadership Network mind-set identifies church leaders with forward-thinking ideas—and helps them to catalyze those ideas resulting in movements that shape the church.

Together with HarperCollins Christian Publishing, the biggest name in Christian books, the NEXT imprint of Leadership Network moves ideas to implementation for leaders to take their ideas to form, substance, and reality. Placed in the hands of other church leaders, that reality begins spreading from one leader to the next . . . and to the next . . . and to the next, where that idea begins to flourish into a full-grown movement that creates a real, tangible impact in the world around it.

**NEXT: A Leadership Network Resource
committed to helping you grow your next idea.**

leadnet.org/NEXT

With deep gratitude
to
Doug and Sherry Bennett
Who have prayed for me for more than twenty-five years
and
John Maxwell
Who has mentored and believed in me for
more than thirty-eight years

CONTENTS

CONTENTS

PART 3: DAILY PRACTICAL DISCIPLINES

FOREWORD

When Dan told me he was writing a book that will help leaders develop confidence, I quickly became very interested. In over fifty years of developing leaders, I have learned that very few leaders are *naturally* confident, and even less are *consistently* confident.

My work with leaders is international in scope, and I'm privileged to teach thousands of leaders every year, as well as coach the top leaders of corporations, churches, and governments around the world. Lack of confidence is universal. There are a few who are naturally, authentically, and consistently confident, but most benefit from their confidence being developed.

Here's what I see. Leaders are passionate; they possess vision. Leaders are smart; they know how to think. Leaders are hungry; they want to grow. Leaders work hard; they are willing to pay the price. Yet, despite all these positive attributes, true confidence seems to be elusive.

Here's how it happens. Problems and pressure are part of the leadership landscape, and inevitably a leader is criticized. Perhaps a prominent person disagrees with your decision, or an important group doesn't like the direction you're headed. Whatever the situation, your confidence is shaken. Perhaps a new program doesn't work, or church attendance drops, or you don't raise the money you need. Your confidence takes a hit. Maybe a key staff member leaves or a new idea fails. You get the idea. It's a natural process, but it leads you to second-guess yourself, and your confidence falters.

The normal response is to fake it. It is true that there are times you must suck it up and keep leading. But you can only do that for so long. The next attempt might be to try new and different programs, emulate a better leader's teaching style, or get a new strategy. These kinds of things are often helpful and can boost your confidence, but they are not the real long-term solution. Why? Confidence is an inside job. *Confidence is impacted by external circumstances, but it is improved by internal processes.*

Here's what I want you to know. You can develop your confidence to a higher level. Your confidence can become more authentic and function on a much more consistent basis. And you can do it by being yourself, just the way God made you.

Dan is a good example. He's always had confidence about life in general. But when I met him, he was a mix of underconfident and sometimes overconfident leader. He was underconfident in ways that made him unsure of himself at times, and occasionally, he was overconfident simply because he lacked experience. I've watched his confidence grow over the last thirty years to a point where now thousands of leaders across the country look to him for wisdom and leadership coaching. This book isn't about Dan, but I can see the process he has gone through within its pages.

You may be overconfident or you may lack confidence; either way it will get you into trouble. Whether an oversized ego or insecurity, either one will prevent you from leading at your full potential. That's why I love this book. My passion is to add value to people, and this book will add value to you and those you lead.

Here's what I hope you will do. Read this book and take the principles seriously. Don't skim the pages; dig in and take a deeper look. *Confident Leader!* will make a difference in your life.

Allow me to be candid as I close. You may say that your confidence comes from God, and ultimately that's true if you are a person of faith. But we are human beings, and God granted wisdom to others who will help you process and develop something deeply personal and incredibly important: your own personal leadership confidence.

I can't wait for you to read this book.

John C. Maxwell
Bestselling author, leadership expert, motivational
speaker, and leadership mentor to thousands

INTRODUCTION

CONFIDENCE MAKES LEADERSHIP BELIEVABLE

As a kid, I remember skipping rocks across the water. It was so much fun, yet also really frustrating. Sometimes I threw the rock and it would hop and glide across the water effortlessly and endlessly. I remember thinking, *That one's going forever!* Then other times it would hit the water and sink . . . like a rock.

Still, something about the simple act of skipping a rock draws you back to keep trying again and again. *The next one will be perfect,* you keep saying to yourself. And when you finally throw one just right, the smile it brings makes all the effort worth it.

Successfully skipping a rock can seem like a mystery that few have solved. Is it a gift for a select few or something that everyone can learn and develop? In the same way, leadership confidence is like skipping a rock, and we wish someone would teach us the secret.

Some leaders throw the rock too hard, confident—sometimes overconfident—that the rock will fly across the water. But instead it hits the water like a brick and sinks. Then there are leaders who throw the rock too softly without enough inertia for it to ever begin its glide. They're too tentative, unsure how to throw it, so the rock never gets the opportunity to fly.

Everyone knows that when you skip a rock it won't go on forever, but that's not really the point. The real question is, How far *can* it go?

Isn't that what we as leaders are always asking? How far can the vision go? How many people can we reach? How well will our church grow? How many lives can we change?

Leadership isn't a one-time event. It's a fluid process with changing conditions. Sometimes the water is choppy, and sometimes it is smooth like glass. Sometimes you throw just a little too hard, and other times you don't give it quite enough force to get it going.

Over the course of more than three decades of ministry and thousands of conversations with church leaders, I've discovered that the majority of leaders do not maintain a consistent quality of confidence. Their confidence goes up and down too easily, impacted by a wide variety of factors, such as personal performance, size of the church, belief in self, support from others, approval from others, mistakes made, and trust and reliance on God.

Questioning one's confidence is a practical and common experience. Here are a few everyday examples:

- As you develop your next sermon, you wonder if it will connect with people.
- As you think about a big staffing decision, you waver, feeling uncertain the candidate is the right person.
- As you set next year's budget, you question whether that much money will come in.
- As you pray about a difficult and confrontational conversation, you second-guess your position.
- As you prepare to communicate a new vision, you doubt if God has really confirmed it.

In each of these examples, a clear and authentic confidence is invaluable to your leadership. The fifteen chapters in this book offer you a process by which you can develop a more consistent and authentic confidence that will serve you well as a leader. There honestly is no secret, and the concepts will break down any illusion of mystery.

Confident Leader! is organized into three parts that build upon each other:

- Part 1: Deep Foundational Decisions—There are specific decisions you can make that establish stability and certainty in knowing who you are and how you were designed to lead at your best. These decisions set the foundation of your confidence.

- Part 2: Deliberate Character Development—Your character is at the core of your confidence. The stronger your character, the greater your confidence. I address five specific areas of your character that will strengthen your confidence.
- Part 3: Daily Practical Disciplines—There is a direct connection between competence and confidence. However, you can be competent, yet not confident. And you can be confident, yet not competent. Both are needed together. I focus on five essentials that you will need to become an effective leader and increase your confidence.

Together, these three parts form a road map for you to move from being either overconfident or underconfident to authentic confidence. To understand this more clearly, let's define each of these concepts briefly here. (We'll address these in greater detail in chapter 1.)

- Being *overconfident* is a result of estimating your abilities to be greater than what they really are. It lacks self-awareness and connection to the practical evidence that supports what God wants to do in and through you.
- Being *underconfident* is a result of believing less in your abilities than God does, being swayed by the opinions of others, and being unduly influenced by fears, insecurities, and failures.
- In contrast, *authentic confidence* is a grounded assurance of your thoughts, decisions, and actions based on a reliance on God's presence and power. An assurance that is combined with an acceptance, appreciation, and cultivation of the gifts and abilities God has given you.

The essence of leadership involves the unknown. If you're truly out in front leading and taking new territory, you will absolutely experience uncertainty. Making measurable progress in leading others to places where you and they have not traveled before creates questions, doubts, and wavering confidence. Because of this, most leaders struggle with being either overconfident or underconfident. My leadership journey, like others, has contained seasons of both.

Every leader longs for authentic confidence. This book uniquely addresses the essentials of such confidence and provides a practical guide to help you consistently develop and maintain it.

I pray this book is a blessing to you as you seek to glorify Jesus through your leadership.

PART 1

DEEP FOUNDATIONAL DECISIONS

*You begin to build a better life by determining to
make good decisions, but that alone is not enough. You
need to know what priorities to set for your life.*
—JOHN C. MAXWELL

When our family moved from San Diego to Atlanta in 1997, we discovered that Chick-fil-A was almost a religion in the Southeast. It's so wildly popular that almost immediately new friends served it at a meeting. Innocently I asked, "I've never heard of Chick-fil-A before. Is it good?" I thought they were going to blindfold me and quietly put me on a bus back to Southern California.

You are probably among the tens of millions who recognize the brilliant and playful slogan Eat Mor Chikin, uttered by black and white Holstein cows pleading with us to make a change in our choice of meat. Chick-fil-A is, by every measure, a highly successful company that operates more than twenty-two hundred restaurants in forty-six states and counting.[1]

Yet more important than any marketing campaign is what's behind the business that made it so successful. Truett Cathy, founder of Chick-fil-A, began his business in Hapeville, Georgia, on May 23, 1946. Few people know he originally named it the Dwarf Grill, and later, the Dwarf House.

It wasn't until 1967 that Truett opened the first Chick-fil-A restaurant in Atlanta.[2]

Back in 1946, Truett made the foundational decision to close on Sundays. Having previously worked seven days a week in restaurants that were open twenty-four hours, he saw the importance of closing on Sundays so his employees could set aside one day a week to rest, enjoy time with family, and worship if they choose—a practice still upheld today.[3] Early in Chick-fil-A's growth, this decision prevented them from becoming established in several prime mall locations. Regardless of the sales growth that opening on Sundays might have generated, Truett held firm to his conviction.[4]

Since then, it's become obvious that Truett's decision not only didn't hurt Chick-fil-A's bottom line, but it actually greatly enhanced its success. Ultimately, the mall representatives learned that Chick-fil-A produced as much sales in six days as their other tenants did in seven. And in nearly every case, Chick-fil-A had the highest volume of sales out of all the food tenants in the mall.[5]

Truett Cathy's early leadership established a culture and a set of values that have endured and continue to inspire their loyal employees and customers to this day. That culture was so strong and enduring that, in 1982, these words were crafted to reflect their purpose statement: "To glorify God by being a faithful steward of all that has been entrusted to us. To be a positive influence on all who come in contact with Chick-fil-A."[6]

On a visit to their corporate headquarters in Atlanta, I saw that purpose statement carved in stone and placed on the front door. You could sense the history, the commitment, and the respect. It was a very cool moment.

Foundational decisions open the door for other factors of success as well. For example, Chick-fil-A is known for its hospitality and the famous line: "My pleasure." What makes that statement so powerful is that it's genuine, and it's genuine because it's part of the culture. This is a direct result of Truett's commitment and desire to serve and have a positive impact on people's lives.

Foundational decisions ring true because they come from personal conviction. Truett's final step in his Five-Step Recipe for Business Success states, "I was not so committed to financial success that I was willing to abandon my principles and priorities. One of the most visible examples of this is our decision to close on Sunday. Our decision to close on Sunday was our way of honoring God and of directing our attention to things that mattered more than our business."[7]

The power of foundational decisions can change the course and outcome of your life, your church, or your business. A foundational decision is one that is intentionally set with the fullness of mind, heart, and soul. It is sustained with strong conviction and a willingness to pay the price. It also shapes your values, impacts your actions, and in great part, helps determine your destiny.

The next five chapters will offer you the opportunity to think through and embrace specific life-changing decisions that will increase your leadership confidence.

CHAPTER 1

OWNERSHIP

TAKE CHARGE OF YOUR LEADERSHIP CONFIDENCE

*Twenty years from now you will be more
disappointed by the things you didn't do than by
the ones you did do. So throw off the bowlines.
Sail away from the safe harbor. Catch the trade
winds in your sails. Explore. Dream. Discover.*
—MARK TWAIN

The first sermon I ever delivered taught me a lot about confidence. I felt prepared as I stepped up on the platform with my Bible in hand. I was ready. In fact, I couldn't wait. I had prayed hard, studied diligently, and had my notes down pat. The cherry on top of all my preparation was an incredibly encouraging senior saint and prayer warrior named Jenny, who was cheering me on from the front pew. Everyone loved to be around Jenny, because she always made you feel better about being you. I felt confident.

Then something happened I had not anticipated. I stepped up on the stage and stared at a hundred pairs of eyes staring right back at me—the guy in charge of the moment. I was the leader for the next thirty minutes. From there, I have no idea what happened. Everything went kind of gray and all sense of confidence left me. I know I said something, because twenty-five minutes evaporated quickly (much like my confidence), and I was pretty sure it did not go well. My intuition was soon confirmed by one of the sweetest, most godly women in the world.

Jenny jumped up to greet me with her angelic smile. Her eyes sparkled with genuine love as she grabbed both of my hands, looked into my eyes, and exclaimed with a big smile, "Dan, your *next* sermon is sure to be better!"

I never felt so wonderful about feeling so terrible in my life. But Jenny could do that. She was an amazing encourager.

I should not have been too surprised. After all, I had just graduated from college with a major in criminal justice administration. That should have been my first clue; I was a private investigator, not a preacher. But I had been a Christian for five years and had watched how the preaching thing was done. It looked easy enough, right? Further, I had served as the leader of the college ministry in a much larger church for about four years. My confidence and passion were strong. However, that was under the close mentoring of the college pastor, and I was a volunteer leader. Here's what I've learned: the moment you step up to lead, you immediately become aware of your level of confidence. No amount of imagination, preparation, or anticipation can replace action.

> The moment you step up to lead, you immediately become aware of your level of confidence.

My false sense of confidence led to overconfidence, and that led to what must have been as painful a thirty minutes for the small congregation as it was for me. Fortunately, that experience didn't shake my calling to ministry. But it was a long time before I ever stepped up to preach again. My confidence had taken a hit.

This story demonstrates a reality of leadership confidence. There is an ebb and flow to it, in the moment as well as through the seasons and stages of your leadership career. This is especially true in the early stages, but veteran leaders experience ups and downs in confidence as well. For example, when a major change takes place, the newness can shake your confidence with the disruption it brings. And of course, when mistakes and failures happen it's common that your confidence may be challenged.

Leadership confidence is not a constant, and it's not guaranteed once you have experienced it. However, your confidence as a leader can be developed. And through the process of intentional development, it can become remarkably consistent and able to weather even the most difficult storms.

Moses: The Reluctant Leader

Leaders often struggle with questions, such as: Am I good enough? Do I have the charisma to inspire others to follow me? Will they listen to me? What if I fail? Or perhaps they worry they're not qualified to truly effect change, which can lead to the question, Does what I do matter?

As I read the Bible, Moses stands among the best leaders of all time. Yet he clearly did not start out that way. He was reluctant to lead and lacked confidence; he tried to get out of leading by telling God he was not a good speaker; and he worried that the people would not believe him or listen to him (Exodus 3–4).

Moses had to make a deep foundational decision. Would he follow God's leadership calling and trust him when he was not confident to lead? A brief recounting of Moses' story across the first five chapters will bring insight and illustration to your study, practice, and development of leadership confidence.

MOSES' DECISION TO LEAD

Moses was raised in the lap of luxury. Rescued from the Nile River as a baby by Pharaoh's daughter, he spent his life as a young man in the palace as part of the royal family. He grew up knowing power, prosperity, and privilege. Josephus and other ancient historians say that Moses was afforded every comfort that members of Pharaoh's family enjoyed and had no need to involve himself in the problems of others.[1] However, when Moses was still a baby,

Pharaoh's daughter said to Moses' mother, "'Take this baby and nurse him for me, and I will pay you.' So, the woman took the baby and nursed him" (Exodus 2:9).

During these formative years, Moses stayed connected to his family, and Scripture indicates that after moving into Pharaoh's palace, he remained keenly aware of his Israelite heritage (Exodus 2:11). As a man, he became acutely aware of not just the existence of, but the pain of, his Hebrew brothers and sisters as they struggled and suffered under their Egyptian slave masters.

Moses became burdened by their burdens. Yet in Acts 7:23, it says he took no action until he was forty years old. So what was going on inside him before then? For a time, he probably dismissed the oppressive culture around him as just the way things were. Eventually, though, there was a moment when he found himself suddenly awakened to the possibility that things were not as they should be, and that he might be called to do something about it— that perhaps he had been saved from the river for a purpose greater than he could conceive.

Still, what could he do? He was just one man. He wasn't Pharaoh. How could he possibly have enough confidence to change all of Egypt? A growing internal conflict rose within him as the stark contrast between his life of ease and his people's hardship gnawed at his soul.

One day, he went to visit his people and saw an Egyptian overseer mercilessly beating a Hebrew slave. In that moment, something inside him changed. He decided to act because he could no longer just consider the idea of leadership; he had to take ownership of it.

While some may not consider his killing of the slave master as the best response, it is clearly the first time Moses owned his responsibility and took action. He had just moved from passive observer to leader. Whether Moses realized it or not, the path to becoming a confident leader begins with a decision.

Your Leadership Journey Is Unique

Every leader's story is different, but the path to confidence is very similar. You may relate to Moses' reluctance and lack of confidence, or you may be overconfident at times. Regardless of your unique design, the process of developing your confidence to its most mature and consistent state is navigated in part by how intentionally you take ownership of it.

The first foundational decision, after your decision to lead, is to take charge of your confidence. Over the course of my ministry career, I have been fortunate to work closely with three senior pastors who did just that. Each is an extraordinary leader, and their stories are quite different, as is the manner in which their confidence is demonstrated.

Bold Confidence

John Maxwell is my long-time friend and mentor. He is also a world-class leader. In 1969, he became the senior pastor of his first church, which was located in Hillham, Indiana. It was a small country church, but John's enthusiasm as an evangelist was high and his confidence as a leader was strong.

One fall, John had set a huge attendance goal of 300. No one in that little country church believed it was possible. But on that first Sunday in October they had 299. John stood before the people and told them he would not preach till they had 300 and then left the building. It was a bold move. He walked across the street to a little gas station and found Sandy and Glen, two guys who never attended church. He convinced them to come with him, and when they walked in, the church went wild. 301! The power of passion and confidence was set in John's heart that day, and he never lost sight of it. The congregation would never doubt God again.

When John and I met in 1982, he was the senior pastor of Skyline Church, then located in Lemon Grove, California. John's charisma, natural leadership, and exceptional communication abilities certainly added to his level of confidence. But his confidence was rooted in a highly intentional focus on personal growth and years of experience beginning back in Hillham.

I joined his staff as an intern and years later became his executive pastor.

As our relationship grew closer, I began to understand that John's confidence came not only from his natural ability and remarkable leadership, but his trust in God and love for people shaped and matured his confidence over the years. Today, John's confidence remains bold and strong, and it is enhanced by his wisdom and generosity.

Quiet Confidence

Andy Stanley is the founding and senior pastor of North Point Ministries. My wife, Patti, and I started attending its Alpharetta campus when we moved from San Diego to Atlanta in 1997 with INJOY, one of John Maxwell's former ministries. Andy is a brilliant leader. He has a love for the unchurched and is one of the most gifted communicators I know.

We attended North Point for weeks before I knew who Andy was. This was partially because in those early days, the creative approach to Sunday was focused on children, and parents were invited. We had two young children then, and we loved it. Adult worship services were every other week on Sunday evenings, but we had not yet attended.

The other reason we didn't know Andy was because he possessed a quiet confidence that was strong and sure but didn't call attention to himself. He was always present at the Sunday morning program, but I didn't know that until we were introduced by Reggie Joiner, the former executive director of family ministries.

My opportunity to serve as an elder on the board at North Point allowed me the privilege to get to know Andy as a person and a leader. One evening in Andy's home with a group of leaders he had gathered, I took a moment after most of the leaders had left to ask him, "Did you ever dream God would do all this at North Point?" Without an ounce of pride, he quietly and humbly said, "Yes, I always knew God would do something big." He added, "That doesn't necessarily mean size, as in attendance like we normally think, but like something big for the kingdom." It turned out to be both. Andy's quiet confidence and great faith in God was evident then and still is today.

Layered Confidence

Kevin Myers is the founding and senior pastor of 12Stone Church in Atlanta, Georgia. In 1987, Kevin and Marcia confidently left their home in

Grand Rapids, Michigan, to move to Atlanta to follow God's lead. Their dream and vision were to plant a church specifically focused on reaching the lost. The early years were filled with hope and potential, but they were also filled with difficult struggles. For the first five years the church met in a variety of buildings, from a movie theater to a Jazzercise facility. Throughout that time the attendance remained at fewer than eighty people. Kevin's confidence was shaken by the lack of growth.

Kevin and I met years later in 1997, when Patti and I moved to Atlanta and made a few visits to his church to see what he and God were up to. The church, then named Crossroads, had grown considerably in great part because of Kevin's compelling and gifted leadership and love for the lost, in addition to his dedication to prayer. Kevin is the first leader I've ever known to pray with an actual sword. He often says, "You just can't pray casually with a sword." His confidence was restored and growing through prayer.

I joined his team as executive pastor in 2001. It was then that I got to know Kevin on a personal level and began to appreciate his confidence as a leader. It quickly became obvious that he was a strong and godly leader, gifted communicator, and creative visionary. But the true reason for his growing confidence had always been his reliance on God.

God helped Kevin build his leadership confidence layer by layer. I liken it to the process of laying bricks one at a time to construct a strong building. Their partnership continues to this day through a journey of more than thirty years in one church. I'm also grateful for our ministry partnership and friendship as well.

Your Leadership Confidence

How would you describe your leadership confidence? Is it higher or lower than a year ago? Would you describe it as consistent or up and down? Growing or fading? As for the style of confidence, would you say yours is bold, quiet, or layered? There is great freedom in your personal style of confidence; there is no right or wrong way to be confident. Ultimately, it's about whether *you* are confident, and others sense it. The good news is that you can develop your leadership confidence. Here are the first three steps to take.

1. Embrace Your Calling to Ministry

We are all called to one of two main categories of ministry (Ephesians 4:11–12). One category is for Christians God has designed and gifted for work in the marketplace. Keep in mind that the vast majority of Christians will not be in full-time ministry but will serve in their church and have influence where they work. This is a profoundly important calling with potential for significant and lasting kingdom impact within the business arena.

The other category is full-time vocational ministry. Full-time local church ministry is not an easy road, so do not chase it lightly. But it is an incredibly fulfilling and rewarding one when you know it is God's plan for your life. I consider myself blessed beyond measure to have been in full-time ministry now for thirty-nine years.

For either category, your call to ministry may come in a moment or it may require a long, deliberate process. It may be ignited from an extraordinary and inspirational experience or begin in quiet obscurity. For some it's embraced quickly, and for others, like me, it is resisted for a time.

Understanding your leadership calling helps you embrace it. There are three important confirmations that help you gain clarity and certainty about your call to ministry.

- *Hearing the voice of God.* God delights to reveal his purpose and plans for you. He speaks and makes himself clear. In my experience, it's more of a "quiet thought" that over time has become his recognizable voice. It's the gift of the Holy Spirit through a clear prompt. With time and experience, you will know that thought came from God—that it was his voice. Commit yourself to sitting in his presence and earnestly listening for him to speak. Ask him what his plans are for you. He will make them clear.
- *Receiving affirmation from the leaders above you.* The leaders above you have been placed there for a reason. You may not always understand the process of their selection and might even disagree at times, but for there to be order over chaos, there must be authority.

  Those in authority carry the responsibility of the organization's mission and your growth as a spiritual leader. Your best interest should be their intent. With this in mind, it is important for you to seek the affirmation of those above you for your leadership in ministry. If they are hesitant, or they tell you "not now," it is important to listen, discover why, and ask for a growth plan. The best way to rise to leadership is to follow well, learn quickly, and serve with a great attitude.

- *Seeing the results of your leadership.* In John 15:1–5, Jesus describes the results of leadership as fruit. In verse 8, he says, "This is to my Father's glory, that you bear much fruit, showing yourselves to be my disciples."

On a practical level, this means you are able to build something and see lives changed as a result. For example, let's say you are selected by a leader in your church to lead a small group, and you begin that group with seven people. That's a great start. If you have ten people by the end of the semester and you can tell a couple of stories of changed lives, that is

> For there to be order over chaos, there must be authority.

spiritual fruit. That is a positive, confirming result of your leadership. If you do not immediately see fruit, however, you may just need more time, coaching, and development. It doesn't mean you are not a leader.

2. Accept Your Leadership Responsibility

I began this section by saying we are all called to ministry. Then, I introduced the idea of receiving affirmation of your leadership. It may be unexpected but there are called, gifted, and affirmed leaders who choose not to lead. They just say no. This should not be too surprising. Even Moses attempted to say no.

Just because you have influence doesn't mean you use it for a purpose or for God's plan. You must personally accept it. It's up to you how you grow and use your influence—for God's plan or yours.

Once you understand your calling, have been affirmed in your leadership, and begin to see results, the reality of accepting that leadership becomes more tangible. You begin to feel the weight and responsibility of the position, along with the affirmation and confirmation.

I knew my calling was to full-time vocational ministry. I heard from God, received affirmation, and saw the results of my effort to serve others. However, when I had been accepted to seminary, at the last minute I withdrew. I said, "No, I'm not going." I did not accept my God-ordained leadership responsibility. The good news is that I didn't run from ministry or the church altogether. My love for the church remained strong.

As I mentioned earlier, I became a private investigator after college. That was the route I took instead of seminary, but I continued to serve as a volunteer leader in the church. There is nothing wrong with that path, except that it was not God's plan for me. It took a little more than a year of wrestling before I surrendered to God's plan. When I called the seminary, they told me, "Good timing, your acceptance is still good for one more day." Had I called two days later, I would have been required to start the long and rigorous process of acceptance all over again. God's patience with me was a great gift.

3. Evaluate Your Current Level of Leadership Confidence

Assessing your own level of confidence as a leader is not always easy. There are a number of different factors in play at any given point in time. For example, being recently released from your job is not a good time to assess your confidence. In contrast, perhaps you just knocked the ball out of the park in a lesson you taught or at an event you led and affirmation abounds. The encouragement is great, but that also may not be the best time for a realistic and accurate assessment.

A better approach is to consider your overall confidence as a leader over a longer period of time. I recommend you review it at least a year, if not two to three years, into your leadership. Reflect on the ups and downs and the failures and successes as you think about how your confidence measured up in each season.

If you are young and new to leadership, you obviously have less experience and time to consider, so just start with the experience you have. The good news is that you are beginning a smart practice early in your leadership.

We could easily break down the many nuances of leadership confidence into a long list, but keeping it simple is always more practical, and it increases our ability to take action. I believe there are three main categories in which we can find and place ourselves: being overconfident, being underconfident, and having authentic confidence. As you think about these categories, make an honest and accurate assessment of your leadership confidence.

- *Being overconfident.* Overconfidence may sound better than underconfidence because having more confidence seems more appealing than lacking it. But you can get into just as much trouble as a leader for being overconfident as underconfident. Overconfidence can stem from pride and lead to arrogance. It can cause you to be cocky and make decisions that lack wisdom. It can also result in controlling others rather than empowering them. Overconfidence is believing more in your own ability than what God can do in and through you.
- *Being underconfident.* In a leader a lack of confidence is more common than having too much confidence, but it is not often admitted. The same fears and insecurities that contribute to the lack of confidence also prevent leaders from owning it. We all have fears and insecurities, but that's different from being a fearful or insecure leader. The important thing is that your growth allows you to overcome your fears and minimize your insecurities as you mature as a leader. We will talk more about that in chapter 2. A lack of confidence can cause you to hold back, become indecisive, and communicate without enough authority. Being underconfident is believing less in your own ability than God does, and less in what God can do in and through you.
- *Having authentic confidence.* There is no perfect formula for leadership confidence. However, it's important to have a working definition in order to make progress and continue to develop your confidence. Authentic confidence is relying on God's presence and power, in combination with an acceptance, appreciation, and cultivation of the gifts and abilities he has given you.

The result of authenticity is an increasingly consistent and strong sense of personal leadership confidence, and this confidence will be sensed as genuine by those you lead. Your confidence will cause your influence to rise, and your responsibility will be to use it to draw even more people to Jesus.

The good news is you can cultivate your confidence. It's not about personality. Rather, it's a process of gaining awareness, experience, and development. Begin by taking ownership of your confidence through its ups and downs and successes and failures. This will cause your influence to rise and help you realize your dreams and vision. But you must believe in yourself and that God is with you.

The good news is you can cultivate your confidence.

CHAPTER 2

BELIEF

OVERCOME THE GREAT CONFIDENCE BREAKERS

The will of God will not take us where
the grace of God cannot sustain us.
—BILLY GRAHAM

My parents divorced when I was eight years old. I still remember the night my dad came into the bedroom my six-year-old sister, Jean, and I shared and brought us out into our small living room. He said, "Kids, I won't be living here anymore, but we'll still see each other sometimes." Neither of us understood what was happening, but we knew it wasn't good—and it didn't seem right. Dad tucked us back into the little set of bunk beds and told us he loved us very much.

We saw Dad every other weekend on Saturdays. He picked us up in his little black Renault and we went to his apartment or the park. Life was different, but we adapted to the new normal. After about a year, we saw him increasingly less, and by the age of ten, I never saw him again. My sister and I learned in our midtwenties he had passed away years ago.

I know this is a sad story, but I'm sharing it with you because it is also a story of great hope for me. I was a quiet kid to begin with, and my parents' divorce certainly did not boost my belief in myself or my personal confidence. But from age twelve through my late twenties, God sent five mentors who chose me. They cared about me and developed me as a leader; and as they poured into me, I grew tremendously.

To be chosen from all the others is a great gift. It's a gift I hope you never overlook and always receive with gratitude. Take a moment to consider the times someone chose you. Think about your job. Of all the people who could have been hired, they chose you. Or maybe you received a special invitation to an incredible once-in-a-lifetime event. And if you are married, your spouse chose you. Patti and I have been married now for thirty-nine years. We smile when we remember that out of everyone, we chose each other.

The fact that you are reading this book indicates a strong likelihood that you were chosen for a position of leadership. Maybe you were selected as a volunteer leader in your church or for a position on staff. Don't take that lightly. At least one person, and probably many more, believe in you. On the days when your confidence may be less than you desire, lean in to their belief in you.

When I was eighteen and a senior in high school, I received another gift: Christ as my Savior. God transformed me spiritually for eternity, and he also transformed my self-belief, so my confidence began to gain great strength. Just a few months later I was asked to assist the pastor leading a large college ministry in the church I was attending. Looking back, it seemed unusual to be a college freshman and a new Christian and be chosen as the chairman of the college group. But God knew what he was doing, and for the next four years I began learning how to lead.

> It's impossible to separate your leadership confidence from the level of belief you have in yourself.

Sometimes it works like that. Someone believes in you before you truly believe in yourself. It's often your parents or it can be a variety of other people, such as a teacher, a pastor, a coach, or even a good friend. Regardless of who it may be, their belief always carries transforming power.

Your story may be very different. Maybe you were an outgoing kid or teenager who excelled at several things from an early age, so your confidence was high. That, too, is a great gift for which to be grateful. The important thing to remember is that it's impossible to separate your leadership confidence from the level of belief you have in yourself.

We see this continue to play out in the life of Moses. Let's return to his story.

MOSES' LACK OF BELIEF

When we left Moses, he had just taken action to own his leadership. In his mind, killing the Egyptian overseer was an effort to protect his people and lead them. Naturally, he expected his people to see his heart and his position within Pharaoh's house, and to respond to him by following his lead.

Yet he soon had his confidence completely shaken. "The next day Moses came upon two Israelites who were fighting. He tried to reconcile them by saying, 'Men, you are brothers; why do you want to hurt each other?' But the man who was mistreating the other pushed Moses aside and said, 'Who made you ruler and judge over us?'" (Acts 7:26-27).

Nothing shakes a leader's confidence like rejection from the people who are supposed to be following you. Moses' response? Fearing Pharaoh would take his life, he fled to the desert. For the next forty years, Moses lived in obscurity and led nothing but a flock of sheep. He must have thought his days of influencing others as he had in Egypt were gone.

Then, one day, God interrupted him at the burning bush. In Exodus 3-4, God called Moses to something higher, something amazing: a leadership position that required enough confidence to stand up to Pharaoh, the most powerful ruler on earth at the time.

But during his four decades in the desert, Moses had apparently lost all confidence in himself. First, he merely asked, "Who am I that I should go to Pharaoh and bring the Israelites out of Egypt?" (Exodus 3:11). God reassured Moses he would be with him, but Moses said, "Pardon your servant, Lord. I have never been eloquent, neither in the past nor since you have spoken to your servant. I am slow of speech and tongue" (Exodus 4:10).

God replied by asking Moses who made his mouth? Moses' unbelief in himself, however, was so great that even after all of God's reassurances, he still said, "Pardon your servant, Lord. Please send someone else" (Exodus 4:13).

Moses' confidence was paralyzed by a lack of belief. Fortunately, God finally broke through. Moses understood he was capable of nothing on his own, and God made it clear he was authorizing Moses to lead his people. This time, Moses believed God would be with him, supporting and guiding him. Through belief in this call, and in beginning to believe in himself, Moses finally regained enough confidence to return to Egypt and confront Pharaoh. *(Moses + aaron)*

People will not follow a leader who does not believe in him- or herself. That is a leadership reality that none of us can escape, and candidly, you don't want to escape it. It's important that you possess a genuine and consistent belief in yourself, but believing in yourself is not intended to indicate self-reliance. That is not how authentic confidence expresses itself. Believing in yourself reflects knowing that God is with you and that you are dependent on him. It's an unshakable belief that you are in this together—and knowing this truth will lift your belief that you can lead.

God Is with You

Personal belief is an essential foundational decision. This decision of belief is rooted to your salvation by faith in Christ, but it goes further. It connects with your call and development as a leader. There are far too many Christian leaders who know God loves them and Jesus died for them but who don't have a strong belief that God is always *with* them as leaders. In fact, they sometimes feel that God has left them on their own. This obviously has devastating effects on their confidence.

Over lunch, a church planter was telling me about his church and how discouraged he felt. As he talked, it became clear to me that he loved his people, served them well, worked hard, and prayed a lot. He also attended every conference he could, read books on leadership, and had a mentor. But nothing seemed to work. The church

> Not every season is one of success, but that does not mean God has left you.

was not growing. He paused, and in a moment of great honesty and vulnerability, he said, "I just don't know if God is with me in this anymore." His confidence was at an all-time low. I asked him how he had felt when he first arrived at the church, and he said his confidence had been high and his vision strong.

All leaders experience setbacks, and not every season is one of success, but that does not mean God has left you. In order to understand this process more fully, we need to begin with the source of the breakdown in believing in yourself and that God is with you.

Overcoming the Two Great Thieves of Confidence

Two weeks before Christmas, our friends Wade and Lisa experienced a robbery. A young man broke into their home while they were away and ransacked their house, going through every drawer and closet. He clogged up their toilet and partially flooded the basement. He took the presents from under the tree, along with whatever he could find of value, and loaded all in their Toyota Corolla. The thief fled, stealing the car packed full of their possessions.

With help from their friends at church they were able to recover relatively quickly, at least in the physical realm. But this experience left them feeling personally violated. It was hard to shake. Wade relayed to me that hearing noises at night, seeing the fear in his daughter, and watching strangers in the neighborhood produced feelings of insecurity and changed his thinking about his ability to protect his family. As a result, he now trains others on how to protect themselves and regain their confidence.

When evil appears and steals from you, everything changes, including how you think. And that is exactly what happened to Adam and Eve in Genesis 3 when the serpent stole their innocence. The result was fear and insecurity. Let's review the story.

The serpent was a deceiver and a thief, and his method was temptation (Genesis 3:1). Adam and Eve gave in to the temptation (Genesis 3:6).

> Then the eyes of both of them were opened, and they realized they were naked; so they sewed fig leaves together and made coverings for themselves. Then the man and his wife heard the sound of the LORD God as he was walking in the garden in the cool of the day, and they hid from the LORD God among the trees of the garden. But the LORD God called to the man, "Where are you?" He answered, "I heard you in the garden, and I was afraid because I was naked; so I hid." (Genesis 3:7–10)

Adam and Eve hid because of their fear and became insecure because they were uncovered. The ultimate outcome was that Adam and Eve's relationship with God was forever changed. We have all experienced this same reality. There is no leader who escapes fear and times of insecurity. Some experience them more than others, but they happen to all of us.

Fear and insecurity are thieves. They are the great confidence breakers that all leaders face. The more you understand about fear and insecurity the better you are able to overcome them.

Overcoming Fear

Fear robs you of confidence and prevents you from leading at your best. Ashley Evans wrote, "The most destructive power of fear is found in its subtle ability to redirect your attention from God to something else."[1] This is because it distracts you from what you were meant to accomplish and focuses your attention on something unproductive like worry or doubt.

> Fear robs you of confidence and prevents you from leading at your best.

In addition, Evans wrote, "People allow themselves to be ruled by fear because it is more predicable than freedom."[2] In other words, we are creatures of habit and our habits feel comfortable and safe. These may include our favorite people, our favorite coffee, or our favorite programs. As leaders, we, too, can become captive to our routines, because routines are more predictable than the uncertainty that comes with the unknown. In effect, you can trade freedom for fear, which then lessens your ability to believe in yourself.

Fear makes us want to control, so at times we prefer what we can control rather than leading into the unknown. This gives the illusion of power but it's actually captivity, because we end up chained to a world of artificial authority. This position of protection is one that lacks confidence.

Four Common Fears Leaders Face

1. *Fear of failure.* I hate spiders. One of my first questions for God will be why he created them. When we moved to Georgia, I met spiders big enough to pull up a chair and have a conversation with me. Not good. My fear of spiders can cause me to stop dead in my tracks. The bigger the spider, the faster I stop.

   Fear of failure does that too. It paralyzes your leadership. It can make you pull back on vision, delay an important decision, or avoid a confrontation. It is invaluable to recognize that failure is not final. In fact, if you learn from what happened, it can be a stepping-stone into a better future.

2. *Fear of rejection.* Like Moses, none of us wants to be rejected by those we are called to lead. If you have ever experienced circumstances like being fired from a job, having a relationship break down, or not making the cut for a team, you understand that those memories can produce fear when facing new or similar situations. As a church leader, it's easy to fear rejection by someone who simply doesn't like you or an outright betrayal by someone you trusted. This often causes you to pull back from relationships and be self-protective. Trusting others, remaining vulnerable, and risking new relationships are essential for confident leadership.

3. *Fear of embarrassment.* Have you ever done karaoke? I have not. It looks like fun, but I truly cannot sing, and I am sure I would look like an idiot if I tried. My friends would love to see me go for it, but

I would be embarrassed. And while you may not relate to having a terribly embarrassing singing voice, I'm sure you know the feeling.

In the same way, when leaders fear embarrassment, they withhold saying what they really think and feel or get defensive for fear of looking foolish. Confidence is required and is vital to your leadership effectiveness. You've got to put your whole heart on the line.

4. *Fear of the unknown.* Ultimately, fear prevents you from moving forward, making progress, and taking new territory. All of which are for the good of the people you serve and at the core of what a leader does: advance toward the vision God has given you. At all costs, you can't let fear stop you.

Four Steps to Help You Overcome Fear

1. *Believe that God is with you.* When you are convinced that God is with you even in the toughest circumstances, your fear begins to subside. When you know you are not alone in your leadership, you lead differently because you have more confidence. Doubt gives fear permission, but belief suffocates fear. Try to remember a time when God abandoned you. I don't believe you can think of one because, even in the most difficult times, God is with you. In fact, his Word repeatedly reminds us of his presence and strength to overcome fear: "Have I not commanded you? Be strong and courageous. Do not be afraid; do not be discouraged, for the LORD your God will be with you wherever you go" (Joshua 1:9).

2. *Accept your God-given authority.* In chapter 7, we will talk in more depth about authority. But for now, it's important to know that when God calls you to lead, he also grants you spiritual authority to do so. Jesus says that all authority in heaven and earth has been given to him (Matthew 28:18), and he commissions us to "go" (v. 19). Jesus is telling us that we are called and sent with his authority; an authority that is loaned to us. We are, therefore, on purpose with his power. This is a tremendous truth that help us overcome any fear we face. With that divine authority we can replace fear with courage and take action.

3. *Meditate on the truth of Scripture.* God has given us his Word, and

through it we can access his heart, mind, and will. He makes his love, wisdom, and purpose clear and available. There are dozens of verses that will help you break free from fear. Take them to heart,

> Doubt gives fear permission, but belief suffocates fear.

meditate on them, and trust God in his truth. Here are three of my favorite verses:

- "The LORD is my light and my salvation—whom shall I fear? The LORD is the stronghold of my life—of whom shall I be afraid?" (Psalm 27:1).
- "So do not fear, for I am with you; do not be dismayed, for I am your God. I will strengthen you and help you; I will uphold you with my righteous right hand" (Isaiah 41:10).
- "For the Spirit God gave us does not make us timid, but gives us power, love and self-discipline" (2 Timothy 1:7).

4. *Take action.* The greatest antidote to fear is action. It may be a tough confrontation with a staff member, a decision involving a huge amount of money, or preaching a truth that may ruffle feathers. Whatever fear you may have, to break through it, you have to step into it.

Overcoming Insecurity

No one wants to follow an insecure leader. But here is the challenge: all leaders have *some* insecurity. For many it might be very little or almost imperceptible. For others, though, it may be significant and noticed by nearly everyone.

Your life in Christ does not remove the potential for insecurity. However, as you mature and find freedom in Christ, it can become a relatively small issue to manage. And as your insecurity decreases, your confidence increases.

I have seen this in my own life. As I have developed and matured as a leader, my insecurities have become minimal. But there are still occasional situations in which my insecurity flares up. This is not uncommon for leaders. Personal doubts creep in, criticisms take their toll, fatigue plays a part; these kinds of things allow you to fall prey to insecurity. The better you are at recognizing the moment you feel insecure, the faster you can overcome it.

Five Everyday Signs of Insecurity

1. *People pleasing.* There might be moments you have difficulty being yourself and you really want people to think well of you. In these situations, you can easily end up trying to make everyone happy. Intellectually you know that is not possible, but your emotions drive you there anyway. This often allows people-pleasing behaviors to slip into your leadership, such as saying what you think people want to hear, avoiding conflict, or being unable to say no. It is far better to be yourself. People like you best and respect you most when you are the real you.

2. *Defensive behavior.* When you get defensive, you are protecting something. This may include your turf, your position, your idea, or something you feel is yours. I served as a consultant for a church working through a staff restructuring process. One talented staff member, like several others, received a new title, a new boss, and a different spot on the organization chart. His job was essentially the same, however, and so was his salary; the change just made better sense for the overall team. But he became openly critical of the entire process and fought the change, which resulted in loss of influence and damaged relationships.

   It is natural to try to protect yourself if you are insecure about what might happen to you, how you may be perceived, or your notion that somehow when the music stops you will have lost ground or been reduced as a leader. But instead of letting defensiveness get the best of you, take a deep breath, count to ten, and wait before you speak. Give it a minute so you don't start digging a hole from which you can't climb out. It's better to wait a day and come back to the conversation. Organize your thoughts and reengage the conversation with a different frame of mind.

3. *Unhealthy competition.* <u>Competition is normal and good,</u> but like anything, it can become unhealthy if combined with insecurity. For example, it's unhealthy when you find yourself unable or unwilling to cheer for a friend, a fellow staff member, a colleague, or a pastor of another church who is experiencing success while you are not. It's natural to want to win and be successful, but unhealthy competition usually comes from insecurity and it will eat your lunch every time. It gnaws at you from the inside so no one can see it, but you feel it, and it makes you behave differently. <u>Learning to cheer for others will help develop your sense of security.</u>

4. *Taking yourself too seriously.* If you are thin-skinned, oversensitive, and unable to laugh at yourself, you will have difficulty as a leader. <u>My advice is to lighten up a bit.</u> We are all imperfect. That is part of what makes us unique and special. While it's not a license to make excuses about our imperfections, it does give us permission to laugh about them.

   I am technically challenged. One day when, in utter frustration, I was about to throw my printer out the window, a staff member walked in, pushed the power button on, and walked out without saying a word. I heard laughter in the hallway and I followed suit, laughing so hard I nearly cried.

   Your work as a Christian leader is serious, but you do not have to take yourself so seriously. A good rule of thumb is to take God seriously and be able to laugh at yourself.

5. *Performance oriented.* The performance trap is easy to step into and tough to get out of. In the local church, a leader can receive considerable praise and reward for working hard, even for overworking. I have fallen into this trap personally—not taking days off, soaking up praise for my work ethic, and neglecting more important priorities for quick successes. This can, and often does, take leaders out.

> The performance trap is easy to step into and tough to get out of.

   If you get caught in the performance trap, you will soon see that no matter what you do, in your mind it's never enough. If you attempt to overcome insecurity with achievement, there is no end to that vicious circle. The good news is you can stop today. Ask a coach to keep you accountable, put boundaries on your schedule, and learn to focus on what is truly important so you can let the rest go. *Remember, your security is in who you are, not what you do.* When you are freed up to be you, you will become good at what you do. You do not need to perform.

Four Steps to Help You Overcome Insecurity

1. *Don't despise your insecurity.* This may sound like a puzzling contradiction, but the greatest trap to fall into is to be insecure about your insecurities. Remember, insecurity is part of our humanity. Just smile, relax, and own it. Even so, do not think that your insecurities are accepted by everyone but you. This does not mean you adopt insecurity as if there is nothing you can do about it. In contrast, owning is the first step to conquering it.

2. *Take a risk and talk about it.* Most of us need a wise and trusted friend or two to help keep our insecurities at a minimum. I know it can be difficult to open up. Trusting someone when you feel vulnerable isn't easy. Owning a weakness or a certain fear may seem counterproductive, but it will bring invaluable clarity and perspective. Take the risk and talk about it with someone who is strong, smart, and cares about you. You don't need to make it a big deal. Just talking about it can free you up in huge ways, because naming your specific insecurities and the real situations in which they surfaced is a big help to overcoming them.

3. *Identify the most common triggers.* If you work on this intentionally, you will soon figure out a couple of situations that have become common triggers for your insecurity. For example, it might be in a meeting when you are asked a question for which you don't have a good answer, and you think that makes you look bad. Or perhaps it happens when you don't receive an invitation for a special event. When you know what your particular insecurities are, they become much easier to learn to anticipate and handle those situations in a better way.

4. *Remember who you are in Christ.* Paul made it clear that we are a new creation in Christ; the old has gone, and the new has come (2 Corinthians 5:17). Redemption restores our relationship with God and has the potential to reduce the insecurity brought on by our separation from God. Jesus restores the broken relationship, that part of our nature that makes us want to hide. Reconciliation does not remove our insecurity entirely, but as we mature spiritually and experience genuine freedom in Christ, insecurity is no longer a driving force within us and our confidence increases significantly. Your relationship with Jesus provides great power to overcome insecurity.

Belief in yourself and belief that God is with you will help you believe you can lead effectively. This belief is an essential element of your leadership confidence, and it leads to a better understanding of your identity.

CHAPTER 3

IDENTITY

VALUE FIRST WHO YOU ARE, THEN WHAT YOU CAN DO

Without knowledge of self there is no knowledge of God.
Without knowledge of God there is no knowledge of self.
—John Calvin

How do you know if there is a blind spot in your ability to see yourself accurately?

Simon Fuller created the popular television series *American Idol* based on the idea of a live-format singing competition. The program launched its first season in June 2002 and ran for fifteen straight seasons. After one year off the air, it returned for its sixteenth season in March 2018.[1]

American Idol launched the careers of superstars such as Kelly Clarkson, Carrie Underwood, Jennifer Hudson, Adam Lambert, and Chris Daughtry, among many others. *Idol* alumni are responsible for 13 Grammys, more than 61 million album sales, 47 platinum records, 95 gold records, 444 Billboard number one hits, 257 million digital downloads, 2 Golden Globes, and an Academy Award.[2]

The show's concept involved discovering unsigned, unknown singing talents. The contestants were judged by celebrity singing artists and voted on by American viewers. The announcement of the new American Idol at the end of each season was a great culmination, and it launched the winning artist onto a potentially great career.

An intriguing part of the show included the many contestants who tried out but didn't make it. Some were genuinely terrible. This part was sometimes viewed as entertainment and may even have made people laugh, but other times it was awkward, making viewers hope it would just stop. The interviews immediately following the failed auditions often revealed a complete lack of self-awareness.

Many contestants truly believed they could sing really well. They had a gigantic blind spot they couldn't see and were therefore crushed. They believed in their ability so strongly they were convinced they not only should have passed the audition but would likely have won the title "American Idol." Their parting comments often went something like, "I know who I am, and this is what I was born to do."

Each one had constructed an identity that was contrary not only to who they were as a person but also completely disconnected from the reality of their abilities. This is an issue that gets leaders into trouble as well.

How Do You See Yourself?

Once, during a coaching session with a student pastor, it quickly became obvious he did not see himself clearly. Ken had dreams and desires that did not align with his abilities and wiring. He was a bright guy with plenty of passion, but he saw himself as a great communicator when the truth was he was a great administrator. This lack of self-awareness was starting to get him into trouble. Ken was trying to build the student ministry on his teaching, and it was not working, but he just could not—or did not want to—see it.

When confronted with this, his confidence took a nosedive and he doubted his calling. It took almost a year for him to become secure in who he was in Christ and to get comfortable

> Understanding who you are, how you are seen by others, and what you were designed to do is foundational for leadership confidence, and ultimately for leadership effectiveness.

with his crazy-good organizational skills. From there, Ken's ministry began to grow.

Understanding who you are, how you are seen by others, and what you were designed to do is foundational for leadership confidence, and ultimately for leadership effectiveness. As we return to the unfolding narrative of Moses' life, we can see the emerging formation of his true identity. Moses began to see himself accurately, and because of this, his confidence in his ability was rising.

Without this basic foundation, your leadership confidence will always tend toward overconfident or underconfident, and consistent, authentic confidence will elude you.

This is a question Moses likely kept asking himself: "Where do I belong and what does God want me to do?" In the narrative, we can see that God was dealing with Moses' insecurity and helping him see what he was designed to do.

MOSES' IDENTITY AND ROLE

At the burning bush, God revealed that Moses was to return to Egypt to confront Pharaoh and lead his people, Israel, into freedom. This was a Herculean task. Yet, before Moses approached Pharaoh or the decree of the plagues, Moses was still full of insecurity. He said to the Lord, "Since I speak with faltering lips, why would Pharaoh listen to me?" Moses said this to God three times (Exodus 4:10; 6:12; 6:30). His confidence was clearly lacking.

God responded, "See, I have made you like God to Pharaoh, and your brother Aaron will be your prophet" (Exodus 7:1). When God said, "I have made you like . . ." he meant that no matter who he sent to help Moses, including his own brother Aaron, Moses himself would remain God's messenger and leader, even though he had not yet fully accepted that divinely appointed role.

God gently coached Moses through the first plagues of blood, frogs, and gnats. He told Moses, "Go tell Pharaoh," and then, "Tell Aaron to stretch out his staff . . ." (Exodus 7:19; 8:5, 16). The third plague was the *last* time Aaron's staff was used to invoke a plague. By the sixth plague of boils, God said to Moses and Aaron, "Take handfuls of soot... and have Moses toss it into the air" (Exodus 9:8). God was finished with pretense. Moses was the leader, not Aaron.

Following that, God always commanded Moses (no longer Aaron) to stretch out his staff to bring each plague (Exodus 9:22; 10:12, 21), and his comfort with his role simultaneously grew. By the last curse, the death of the firstborn, all of Moses' timidity and fear was gone. He was bold and strong, and even dared fury at Pharaoh for his hard-heartedness (Exodus 11:8). His confidence as a leader had matured.

The pinnacle, of course, was that incredible moment when Moses raised his staff over the Red Sea and watched as God parted the very waters before them. He knew God was doing it, not himself, so there was no misguided arrogance. Yet, he knew if someone else had raised their staff, no waters would have parted. For him, this ability to perform was simply the confirmation of his calling in God, not its foundation. Due to that miracle, Scripture says, "the people feared the LORD and put their trust in him and in Moses his servant" (Exodus 14:31).

Moses was finally aware of his true and fullest identity and role: friend of God and leader of the people of Israel.

Settle Your Identity

Your identity is a significant element of your confidence as a leader. It involves, like Moses, who you are and what you do. Moses was a friend of God (Exodus 33:11). That's who he was. In fact, their relationship was so intimate that the verse begins by saying they spoke "face to face." Who you are always precedes what you do. God's desire is first for you to become the right person, then assume the right role. God had a role for Moses. He called, equipped, and empowered him to be the leader of Israel. That's what Moses did. There is a connection between who Moses was and the role God had chosen for him. We can call that the fullest expression of Moses' unique destiny.

Moses had been wrestling with a deep foundational decision. He had to decide whether he would assume his full responsibility designed by God. But the decision was settled. Moses' trust and faith in God grew enough to realize greater confidence in his own personal identity. This allowed Moses to become the leader he was designed and destined to be.

> Your identity is a significant element of your confidence as a leader.

This same foundational decision involves whether you will pursue and embrace your God-designed identity and role as a leader. The practical path includes three elements. First, you must understand your identity in Christ. Second, you must see yourself accurately. And third, you must embrace a convergence of role and relationship.

Spiritual Awareness

How you see yourself is incredibly important. Therefore, self-discovery in order to understand yourself more accurately is a healthy aspiration.

Self-discovery is a fascinating process, and often includes taking a variety of eye-opening personality tests. We may discover that we're an ENTJ, a Maximizer, a Lion, a high D, a Harmonizer, an Introvert, or that we have "woo."

In a recent job interview, we closed the conversation, prayed, and stood up to leave when the candidate said, "Oh, and I'm an 8." There was no other explanation, and I had no clue what he meant. I later learned that number was connected to the type indicator for the Enneagram.

These assessments are very helpful, but on their own they are limited if you do not first have an accurate biblical understanding of what God thinks about you: your true identity.

The following is a biblical outline of what God thinks about you. This is not a comprehensive list, but it contains the foundational truth about who you are as a Christ-follower:

1. *You are loved and valued.* God loves you unconditionally and his love is unending. God loves you so much that he gave his son Jesus

as a sacrifice, so that you could have eternal life (John 3:16; 1 John 4:7–10). You do not have to earn his love; it's a free gift (Ephesians 2:8). You are valuable because God loves you. Do not measure yourself or your worth by the size of your church, your paycheck, or the number of people who follow you on Twitter. You are a child of God (John 1:12; Galatians 3:26).

2. *You are forgiven and a new creation.* Sin separates us from God, but by grace, through your faith in Christ, your sins are forgiven (Romans 3:23–26; Ephesians 1:7–8). There is nothing in your past that is not forgiven. God's grace covers past, present, and future. You are completely accepted by God. You don't need to conform to the world's standards to be accepted—from what you wear to your position of leadership or whom you marry. You are a new creation (2 Corinthians 5:17). You have freedom in Christ to be the real you (Galatians 5:1).

3. *You are capable and gifted.* You are part of a chosen people, a royal priesthood, and a holy nation. God has called you and set you apart for a special purpose (1 Peter 2:9; Ephesians 2:10; Ephesians 4:11–12). You have been chosen and appointed to bear fruit (John 15:16). You have been given spiritual gifts that are unique when in operation by you (Romans 12:4–8; 1 Corinthians 12:4–11). You have been given power to carry the name of Jesus wherever you have opportunity (Acts 1:8). You have been empowered by God's authority, given to his Son, and now to you as a disciple (Matthew 28:18–20).

This is how God sees you. You are complete in Christ. You lack nothing (Colossians 2:10). This is your spiritual identity. And the deeper you embrace it, the more consistent your confidence becomes as a leader. In fact, Scripture says you can do all things through Christ who strengthens you (Philippians 4:13).

> You are part of a chosen people, a royal priesthood, and a holy nation.

This is a mind-blowing identity. This is the foundation of who you are, and it's integral to your confidence as a leader. The richness and depth of your identity in Christ is truly amazing, and it's yours to own and pursue.

Self-Awareness

I can imagine myself as six foot, four inches with a full head of long blond hair and riding a Harley, but that is just not me. I can pretend, but everyone else will know I am not seeing myself accurately. If that happens, they will not know how to interact with me. And I would not be able to lead them because they don't know who they are following.

Seeing yourself accurately is vital to effective leadership and consistent authentic confidence. When you first see yourself as God sees you, then you can begin to gain an accurate grasp of your self-awareness.

Author Michael E. Frisina offered the following definition: "Self-awareness is an honest understanding of your own values, desires, thought patterns, motivations, goals and ambitions, emotional responses, strengths and weaknesses, and effect on others."[3] In a study printed in *Harvard Business Review*, there are two broad categories of self-awareness: internal self-awareness (how we see ourselves) and external self-awareness (how others view us).[4] Essentially, self-awareness is seeing yourself accurately.

As a leader, if you lack self-awareness, you may know how to *do* leadership but not know how to *be* a leader. This combination results in ineffectiveness and sometimes failure. *Doing* leadership involves things like recruiting volunteers, developing strategy, and executing a Sunday service with excellence. *Being* a leader is the more subjective element that includes things such as reading a room, knowing if people like you and trust you, and adding value to the right person in the right moment in the right way. This is much more complex and involves personal awareness to do it successfully.

The process of gaining a better self-awareness includes self-discovery assessments, coaching with honest feedback, introspection, behaving differently, and most importantly, engaging change. You cannot gain the needed leadership confidence without a willingness and commitment to change to become the most authentic and best version of you.

One of the great values of becoming more self-aware is that it helps you identify and overcome your blind spots. We all have blind spots because we can't see what we can't see. We have limitations and insecurities that, when combined with our dreams and aspirations, can cause us to try to be someone other than our real selves. We then desperately and futilely attempt to achieve the right things in the wrong way because it's not who we really are.

I was coaching a sharp young leader who had tremendous creative, musical, and production abilities. But he lacked self-awareness and had his heart set on becoming an executive pastor. He was absolutely confident he could do it. However, the harder he tried at his current church to do "XP" kinds of things, the more frustrated he became. He had the wrong picture of his skills and wiring. He eventually got hired at another church as an XP but quickly failed out of that job. His confidence took a serious hit. It took months of coaching toward a more accurate picture of himself before he landed a new job as a productive and happy member of the creative team at a large church.

> We all have blind spots because we can't see what we can't see.

Author Terry Linhart wrote: "The foundational reason for examining our lives and blind spots is so we can become more like Christ in our work."[5] This is the connection between your spiritual identity and your self-awareness in the human realm.

The following five areas will give you insights to help you become more self-aware.

1. History

A friend told me a story of his first love in high school that resulted in his heart being broken. As a senior he fell head over heels for a funny, smart, and pretty girl at the school they both attended. They became friends and hung out with a group of classmates together. He was smart and capable but a little on the shy side. It took almost a year for him to muster the courage to tell her how he felt about her. She was kind, but replied, "I care about you, but I don't feel that way about you." This hurt him deeply, and he would tell you that for years that moment affected his confidence and he rarely dated because of it.

You have childhood experiences, memories of your parents, successes and failures, secrets and regrets, joys and best days, report cards from school, your first job, your first kiss, maybe your first child, and so much more. All these things—and more—make up the real you.

The combination of wounds and scars along with successes and highlights have a profound impact on how you see yourself today. The better you understand your past, the more self-aware you become.

2. Emotion

An awareness of your personal history is one of the best ways to help you understand your emotions. Your emotions may run close to the surface, easy for people to see and experience. Another leader on your team may keep her emotions tucked away more privately inside. Neither way is right or wrong. The goal is emotional maturity, which is assessed by how well you respond in everyday situations, ranging from a confrontation at work to playing a board game at home.

For example, let's say you were playing a game and, because you lost, you got angry and refused to play anymore. That is a sign of emotional immaturity. Further, if you think such response is appropriate or can't see how that affects others, you lack self-awareness.

As a leader, are you aware of how you behave when you are hurt, embarrassed, or frustrated? Do you know what makes you angry and how your anger impacts others? Do the people you work with have to walk on egg shells around you, or does your authentic joy draw them closer to you? Your emotional self-awareness is either a great asset or a detriment to your leadership.

3. Motivation

What makes you tick? What fuels you? What gets you pumped up in the morning about the day? Knowing what motivates you is vital to a strong sense of self-awareness. This is especially true in ministry. We are often conflicted by a gap between what we know is the right answer and what we really think, feel, and desire.

A common example is the desire for success. Nearly every Christian leader has a desire to be successful, but some leaders experience inner conflict in at least two realms. First, when they are successful, they feel trapped

> Knowing what motivates you is vital to a strong sense of self-awareness.

between the bookends of pride and humility. They feel good about the success but fear the possibility of pride. This causes them to behave in an awkward and less than authentic manner. Second, they're not sure a desire to be successful is an acceptable ambition for a Christian leader. They, therefore, attempt to over-spiritualize it as God's will or play it down by covering it with false humility.

An accurate awareness of what motivates you allows you to examine that motivation honestly, and determine if you are handling it correctly.

4. Ability

What are you good at doing? What are your strengths and weaknesses? What comes easily and naturally to you, and what do you have to work extra hard to finish?

My friends and colleagues know I'm not so hot at math. Siri and I definitely have a love-hate relationship, and our CFO gives me financial reports in big fonts and fun colors. (Okay, that last part is exaggerated, but you get the idea.) The good news is that I know it. I'm aware of my inadequacy. I don't pretend I know what I'm doing, get defensive, or lean in to those skills for my overall effectiveness. I ask for help and keep learning what I need to know.

If you are a young leader, it's important to give yourself time to learn the things for which you are gifted. Get the honest feedback from those who coach and lead you. As you gain experience, it is vital that you become accurately aware of your true skills and abilities so you can be the most authentic and effective leader possible.

5. Social

Do you know how others perceive you? Let me be blunt and ask you an important question that every leader needs to answer: Do people like you? The next question is even more critical: Do you know why? Understanding social interaction, connection, and how people see you is basic to good leadership. You have, no doubt, met people whom you consider to be clueless about how they behave. They just seem to say the wrong things and generally behave in inappropriate ways. They lack social awareness, which always hurts relationships and is lethal to leadership.

I highly recommend, regardless of your level of experience, that you periodically ask friends who are smart, strong, and love you to tell you the truth. Give them permission to tell you how they and others perceive you. Compare that to how you see yourself. Then go to work on closing the gap and becoming more self-aware.

Awareness Convergence

Awareness convergence is that place where you find the merging of your spiritual identity in Christ, a valid sense of self-awareness, and a connection to your true skills and abilities. This is the birthplace of authentic confidence as a leader, and it gives you clear insight into the following three essentials that are part of the real you:

1. *Personality.* You gain a sense of permission and freedom to first discover the real you, and actually be the real you. There is no need for pretense or trying to be someone you're not. You are always at your best when you are the most real you.

2. *Purpose.* Awareness convergence is the place you begin to sense that you were made on purpose with a purpose. Your calling becomes clearer and your resolve to lead even stronger.

3. *Promise.* Psalm 37:4 is a promise that says, "Take delight in the LORD, and he will give you the desires of your heart." For the longest time I thought that meant God would give me all I dreamed of, longed for, and desired. I have come to understand and believe that was because I focused on the second half of the verse, while nearly ignoring the first part: "take delight in the LORD." I focused on what I wanted and what God would give me, not on my part in taking delight in God by loving and obeying him.

When I "take delight" in God, I am open and receptive to the desires he places within me. These are the best things he has planned for me all along. This does not remove my humanity or free will to choose, but it confirms my identity in Christ and gives me the opportunity to be the person God has designed me to be. The same is true for you.

In the next chapter, we will explore how becoming and remaining attentive to God grants you the most fruitful and confident leadership you can imagine.

> You are always at your best when you are the most real you.

CHAPTER 4

ATTENTIVENESS

HEAR AND HEED GOD'S VOICE

We never grow closer to God when we just live life.
It takes deliberate pursuit and attentiveness.
—FRANCIS CHAN

The daily practice of a three-mile run has been part of my life for a very long time. Wherever I travel, one of the first things I do is scout out my route. From city streets to quiet neighborhoods I have logged a lot of miles. Several years ago, while on vacation with my family in Destin, Florida, I laced up my running shoes and started to head out the door. Patti stopped me and strongly urged me to take some water with me. She warned me how dangerous it was to run in a 94-degree and more than 90-degree humidity weather without water, but I didn't listen. I was overconfident and said, "Aw, I run slow. It's more like a jog; I'll be fine."

I took off running and enjoyed the smell of the ocean. For some unknown reason, when I hit the halfway point of about one and a half miles or a bit more, I just kept going. It seemed like I was channeling my inner Forrest Gump. Somewhere close to four miles out, I was feeling pretty good, but it dawned on me that I now had to jog four miles back. Eight miles is quite a lot when you are accustomed to only three in good weather.

By five miles, I noticed my hands were starting to swell. By six miles, my hands were so swollen the skin felt incredibly tight. By about seven miles, my peripheral vision started to blur, and I became lightheaded and woozy. I knew I was in trouble and would not make it back to the condo. I stumbled into a convenience store and, leaning against the counter, I managed to get out one word: help! The clerk just stared at me. Then a kind and compassionate person came up from behind me, put her arm around my waist, and walked me slowly over to the fountain drink machine. She poured me a cool cup of water and helped me drink. It took fifteen to twenty minutes before I was feeling somewhat normal again. All this because I refused to pay attention to what Patti said to me.

> Remaining attentive to God's voice and close to his heart requires intentional effort.

As a leader for more than thirty years, it hit me how easy and yet dangerous it is to lead without listening to God. It is so foolish to not pay attention to his wisdom and warnings, because we can miss his favor and blessing and even end up in trouble. It is easy to become overconfident, especially when things are going well. You can begin to think, *I've got this.* This does not necessarily come from an arrogant place, but it is self-sufficient, and off you go. It's not intentional on your part, it's just a common response from a leader who is busy, has things to do, and is on the run.

Remaining attentive to God's voice and close to his heart requires intentional effort. It's more than merely your daily prayer, although that's essential. Rather, it's a way of living. Moses demonstrated this foundational decision to remain attentive to God.

MOSES' ATTENTIVENESS TO GOD

Emerging from the Red Sea, Moses' role as the true leader of Israel was not in doubt. But now what? Where do they go from there? A key reason why Moses is recognized as one of history's greatest leaders is not because of what happened at the Red Sea, but because of what he did next. He learned to become deeply attentive to the nature and voice of God.

Moses began this attentiveness with praise for who God is, what God had done, and in recognition that God is the true source of his leadership confidence. Immediately after leading Israel through the ocean, Moses sang, "I will sing to the LORD . . . The LORD is my strength and my defense . . . He is my God, and I will praise Him" (Exodus 15:1–2).

An established leader is soon tested by his or her followers' needs. As Israel moved through the desert, they hit their first obstacle: parched with thirst, but only finding undrinkable water. The people complained bitterly. Moses' reaction? He "cried out to the LORD, and the LORD showed him a piece of wood. He threw it into the water, and the water became fit to drink" (Exodus 15:25).

Moses was confident because he knew where to find answers. Through all the miracles—the manna, the quail, the water gushing from the rock, and more—Moses was attentive to the commands of God, learning to obey his voice. Over and over, Scripture says, "And Moses went up to God," followed by his instructions to the people of Israel "as the LORD had commanded Moses."

And God distinguished him for it. He said to Moses, "Come up to the LORD, you and . . . seventy of the elders of Israel, and worship from afar. And Moses alone shall come near the LORD, but they shall not come near" (Exodus 24:1–2 NKJV). "So, the Lord spoke to Moses face to face, as a man speaks to his friend" (Exodus 33:11 NKJV).

In fact, Moses' only recorded failure was a one-time failure to listen to God. The second time God told Moses to bring water from a rock, he commanded Moses only to speak to the rock, not to strike it. But in an unusual manner, Moses did it his way, striking it and losing the opportunity to lead Israel into the promised land.

Thankfully, this was a one-off. No other mortal man has ever been as attentive to God's voice as Moses. Scripture says, "According to all that the Lord had commanded him, so he did" (Exodus 40:16 NASB).

> **Essentially, the source of our leadership confidence is our relationship with God.**

Spiritually centered leadership is based on a divine partnership with God. He wants us to do what we can do so he is freed up to do what we can't. Essentially, the source of our leadership confidence is our relationship with God. Hearing his voice and acting on it is an essential element to unlocking the authentic confidence God has placed within us. We are tempted to lead on our own when circumstances are going well, but doing so, nearly always ends poorly. The decision to consistently pursue God and remain attentive to his plan is core to our leadership confidence.

It's much easier to talk about having a close relationship with God and being attentive to his voice than it is to live it out in real life, especially when the pressure is on. Yet that's when it counts the most. Kadi's story gives us a glimpse into that reality.

A Conversation with Kadi Cole

Born in Merced, California, Kadi had lived in six states by the time she was six years old because of her dad's military career. She then grew up in the beautiful Rocky Mountains in western Montana. After graduating from college, Kadi took a position as a dean at a Christian university. Then she joined the executive staff at Christ Fellowship Church in South Florida. She served there for sixteen years in a variety of roles, ultimately as the executive director of multisite.

Kadi is a leader of leaders, and consistent success gave her tremendous confidence. Yet, when I asked her to describe her confidence as a leader, she said: "It has grown over time in 'anonymous' ways." She went on to explain that there was a turning point in her story when her attentiveness to God helped bring her to a new level.[1]

At a certain time, while on staff at the church, she found herself stretched in her leadership beyond the point where she could lean on her gifts, skills, and positive personality. She was being pulled in multiple directions. Her husband was struggling with a debilitating chronic illness, and their son was still just in first grade. Her church needed her leadership as much as ever, her husband needed significant care, and her son needed nurturing. It was too much.

To say the least, her natural confidence began to weaken. Her time was exhausted, and so was her body, and she lacked the ability to keep it all together. The tension of the story was still evident in her voice as she asserted: "I was pushed to the outer edges of all my margins—physically, emotionally, intellectually, and even spiritually."[2]

There was a moment in a crucial meeting where she was not prepared and in over her head. Rather than lean in to her abilities, which Kadi knew would not be enough, she surrendered the moment to God. It was as if she and God had walked into the meeting together in genuine spiritual partnership. Kadi sensed his presence and held tightly to that close connection. In the end, it turned out to be more of a miracle than a meeting.

This experience inspired her to move from trusting in the gifts God had given her to trusting God himself to speak through her in the moment. It was a shift in control from herself to God—a different type of surrender, along with no need to prove anything. And it was the emergence of a confidence in God, not in her God-given abilities.

Kadi's comment about her confidence growing in anonymous ways seemed like an unusual word choice, so I asked her about it. She candidly shared that it was not easy growing up as a woman with leadership gifts in an American church. Her gifts were not always appreciated or welcomed. But in school, the community, and among personal friends, her gifts and abilities were encouraged. Accordingly, the term *anonymous* means her confidence grew through informal affirmation.

Kadi learned to look internally to gain her confidence from God. She said, "I've learned not to attach my confidence to the approval and affirmation of others, and not get stuck thinking about the things that are not open to me. I stopped asking myself why I didn't get invited, wondering if I wasn't good enough. This conflict was actually a gift to me because it taught me the value of informal influence over formal organizational position."[3] What great insight! Today, she is the founder and CEO

> Real influence is not bound by organizational structure.

of Kadi Cole and Company, an author, a coach, and a great gift to the Christian leadership community.

Real influence is not bound by organizational structure. Also, it's possible to rise in leadership and still feel less confident in your formal role because of a lack of internal confidence and belief. Whenever you are promoted to a new level, this is always a possibility. It's important to sustain, and even grow, your confidence as you rise within an organization. God is ultimately your source for that confidence.

Four Components of Spiritual Attentiveness

You may be strong, gifted, and confident like Kadi. Maybe you are overconfident, not necessarily in an arrogant way, but perhaps you are tempted to not pay as close attention to God as you should. Regardless of your talent and ability, I think we can all relate to a time when the load was just too much. How about you? How did you handle it? Did you try to pull it off on your own, or did you draw closer to God? What will you do differently the next time the load gets to be too heavy?

The deep decision to remain spiritually attentive is vital to your leadership. The following four components of spiritual attentiveness will greatly help you remain deeply connected to God and increase your confidence as a leader.

1. Desire God

The desire for God is personal. God is not only an entity, deity, and God above all gods; he is a person who feels and thinks. He possesses great love and desires relationship. True attentiveness begins with an awareness of the personal nature of desire he fashioned in us when he made us in his likeness. That sets the stage for how and why you pursue God.

Chasing after God is about wanting him more than success. This does not mean you have to abandon the desire for success as a leader; it means you desire him more. And further, it means you desire him first. Pursuing God demonstrates the intent of your heart and reveals a healthy dependence on him. You recognize that while you are leading, God is with you providing wisdom, power, and favor that you do not have without him. Knowing that adds great strength to your confidence.

Your desire for God keeps you centered and at peace in both times of success and times of pressure, trouble, and even failure. Without an intimate connection, it's easy to think you are the source of success or are personally the failure. This can lead to overconfidence, arrogance, discouragement, or losing your way.

Your desire for God and relationship with him defines your dependence on him. A business owner I recently met talked about how much he remains connected to God through prayer during the ups and downs of leading his small income tax preparation business. In particular, hiring qualified accountants is not an easy responsibility to manage. If you hire too few, they can't meet the needs of the clients and their schedules. If you hire too many, they sit bored without work and end up quitting. The owner hired three new accountants last February but was worried that on their first week there was not one appointment booked. He prayed for well over an hour, and yes, clients called and booked.

> **Your desire for God and relationship with him defines your dependence on him.**

The amazing part is that he said he never prays to get merely what he wants but what God wants. He makes the needs known, but doesn't feel rejected when God answers his prayers differently than what he asked. Clients don't always come in. And if he doesn't get the answer he hoped for, he may be disappointed, but he doesn't blame God. He presses on. He simply wants more of God and is grateful for whatever measure of success in business he helps them achieve.

That's a good lesson for us who lead the church. Do we pursue God to get what we want or what he wants? We certainly have freedom to pray openly and honestly, but ultimately, it's our desire for him that determines the relationship and how we lead.

2. Surrender Your Will

I love guitars. In fact, I have a really cool collection of killer guitars. It's basically my only hobby, and it's just fun. Guitars are personal to me, and each one is unique and special. Even though I am not a very talented player, I still get attached to my guitars. So on the rare occasion when it seems like I need to let one go, it matters. It's like prying a cookie out of a two-year-old's hand.

Well, it happened. God asked me to sell a guitar I loved and give the money to the church. His voice was clear and unmistakable. I remember arguing and telling God, "Any guitar but that one." It was a gorgeous and unique Les Paul. I also told God I loved it and that I could just write a check instead. He said, "I know." It took a while, but I finally took it to a friend who owned a guitar store. It sold in one day.

It's not easy to surrender your will. Whether it's about something that ultimately doesn't matter, like a guitar, or something at the core of leading a local church, your will is a formidable force. Surrendering what matters to you is challenging, but fulfillment always rides on the wings of obedience.

> Surrendering bonds your heart to God's heart.

Jesus modeled surrendering his will to the Father with the greatest sacrifice of all: his life. That will not likely be asked of you or me, but sometimes it feels like it. I remember when God asked me to move from San Diego to Atlanta. That was definitely not what I wanted. But I surrendered, and I am so glad I did. My life and leadership have been blessed without measure. I dearly love San Diego and miss my friends there, but this is where God has placed me. Without that surrender, I would never have experienced the kindness of God to serve at 12Stone Church.

Surrendering bonds your heart to God's heart. It's not based in works of righteousness or a kind of strange ascetic spiritual discipline. Instead, it's about practicing a deep and committed attentiveness to God and what he wants for you. It's a closeness that sets you free for greater things. It also helps you let go of the good things in order to gain the great things.

How about you? Are you surrendering your will to pursue what God wants? Surrender is not only in the big and dramatic moments of life. It's often found in the smaller, hidden, everyday things, like saying you're sorry or asking for forgiveness. Whatever it may be, lean in to what God wants.

3. Connect to the Vine

Jesus said, "I am the vine; you are the branches. If you remain in me and I in you, you will bear much fruit; apart from me you can do nothing"

(John 15:5). Attentiveness requires desire first and surrender second. The third component is connection. To be deeply and consistently connected with God is to abide or remain in him.

Perhaps you are married. Your marriage relationship is legally secure, but there's much more to it if you want to experience all that awaits you. Your relationship will not remain close, alive, and intimate without a consistent heart-level connection. This requires intentionality. It involves having honest conversations, serving each other, making time for each other, sacrificing for each other's well-being, and aligning your will with what you both believe is best for the relationship.

As a leader, your relationship with Jesus is similar. His love for you is forever, and you love him too. But without time, conversation, and intentional connection, the relationship can fade. Worship and your expression of gratitude is also core to the relationship. Praise him for who he is, giving thanks for everything is the best way to set the stage for the most incredible conversation imaginable.

Prayer is the chief conduit for remaining in the vine. It's the primary avenue by which we can say yes to an incredible invitation from God to engage in genuine relationship with him. Prayer is vital in the life of a spiritual leader. Personally, I can't imagine leading, or at least certainly not with confidence, without that connection through prayer. You can pray anytime and anywhere, but it is good to have a special set-aside place if you can.

> **Prayer is the chief conduit for remaining in the vine.**

I had a small prayer room built in our basement, and over the years it has become my favorite place in our home. To me it represents the promise of both God's presence and his power. I know he doesn't reside in my prayer room, but it's a familiar and a special place set aside that helps me focus, listen, and respond. Again, you do not need a prayer room to pray, but it's good to be intentional and invested in whatever helps you stay connected.

Your privilege and responsibility to pray is significant. But keeping it simple is also important. We don't always need apps and notebooks and prayer cards. Don't complicate it. Just sit with God and talk to him. Consider these three points to help you pray:

- *Pray big.* Do not limit the size of your prayers. God can handle whatever you've got. It's God's church, and he placed the vision within you. Praying audaciously is not the same thing as praying foolishly. If my church averaged two hundred in attendance, I'm not going to pray for seven thousand next Sunday. Can God do that? Yes. But that's not the way he has consistently demonstrated his favor. Pray with wisdom, faith, Scripture, and as prompted by the Holy Spirit. But don't be afraid to pray big.

- *Pray specifically.* The more focused, specific, and detailed your prayers are, the more confidence you gain that God answered your prayer and the more inspired you are to pray more. There is nothing wrong with general prayers, but then it's more difficult to know when they are answered. And you might be tempted to think, *Well, it was coincidental that I prayed, and it all worked out.* Praying specifically allows you to celebrate the answers.

- *Pray now.* You may have a favorite place to pray, like I have in my basement, but there is no need to wait to pray until you can get there. Scripture says, "Pray continually" (1 Thessalonians 5:17). That mandate represents having an awareness and engagement in the fact that God is always with you. It's an invitation to pray anytime about anything as the Holy Spirit prompts you. One simple practice I love on Sunday mornings is when someone in the church asks me to pray for them. I ask them if we can pray right then. There is power in that moment.

4. Practice Your Attentiveness and Resolve to Obey

The John 15 passage I mentioned earlier teaches that we are to bear fruit. Jesus goes on to say, "If you remain in me and my words remain in you, ask whatever you wish, and it will be done for you. This is to my Father's glory, that you bear much fruit, showing yourselves to be my disciples" (John 15:7–8).

The phrase "ask whatever you wish, and it will be done for you" is a bold proclamation. It might even sound like an enticing invitation. But I think it's an invitation to practice our faith and leadership. This invitation helps us learn to pray as guided by the Holy Spirit, according to God's will as outlined in Scripture.

I don't pretend to understand the depths of verse 7, but I know that if I'm praying according to God's will, he is in it. Verse 8 then confirms the nature of our prayer by saying it's about the Father's glory, not ours. When my prayers don't seem to be answered the way I prayed, it gives me an opportunity to reflect and learn. I'm actually practicing my attentiveness to learn how to listen and pray more closely in alignment with God's heart. I do not see it as whether I got a prayer right or wrong. It's about making sure I am connected enough to keep walking by faith and leading according to his plan, not mine.

The bottom line is obedience. That does not sound like a relationally oriented word, but when it comes to our attentiveness to God as a leader, there is no escape from obedience. Let's go back to John 15 one more time: "As the Father has loved me, so have I loved you. Now remain in my love. If you keep my commands, you will remain in my love, just as I have kept my Father's commands and remain in his love" (vv. 9–10). We gain an insight here that obedience may be more rela-tionally oriented than it seems. Jesus made a direct connection between our obedience (keeping his commands) and love. We obey because we love him, not because we are forced. We are also attentive to Jesus because we love him, trust him, need him, and choose to follow him. The longer and more consistently we practice this, the stronger and deeper and more authentic our confidence becomes. And the more we practice attentiveness, the more the core qualities of our soul as a leader align with God's heart, which is the focus of the next chapter.

> We obey because we love him, not because we are forced.

CHAPTER 5

SOUL

EMBRACE FIVE CORE QUALITIES
OF CONFIDENT LEADERS

*Strengthening the soul of your leadership is an invitation
to enter more deeply into the process of spiritual
transformation and to choose to lead from that place.*
—RUTH HALEY BARTON

Scientists have long conducted the practice of dendrochronology, the study of a tree's core to determine its age and growth patterns. To oversimplify, a small, thin core is extracted from a tree that generally reveals one ring for each year of the tree's life, but the ring's width reveals much about the conditions where it has grown over time.

Varying conditions, including pollution, erosion, the availability of water, or the presence of fire, determine a tree's growth, health, and strength. These studies give scientists valuable information to estimate future growth in forestry, predict climate changes, and grow healthier, stronger trees.

As leaders, we, too, have a core that reveals much about our health and strength. Our core is the place deep inside that guides how we lead and is, therefore, predictive of our leadership. It's the soul of a leader that contains the qualities that will either draw people to you and increase their trust in you or cause them to move away from you. These qualities can be positive and productive or negative and destructive. You intuitively understand the contrast between being humble or proud, generous or greedy, and courageous or cowardly.

When I refer to the *soul* of a leader, I'm not referring to something only contemplatives would care about or asserting to a specifically theological implication. In this chapter I am referring to the inner qualities that are consistently found in confident leaders, and the soul of a leader is a great word picture of what that entails.

None of us is perfect, but these virtues or attributes are attainable by any leader who chooses to pursue and develop them. These qualities, as I most often refer to them, do not constitute a secret formula for leadership confidence. They are not skills to learn or another list to manage. They are also not something you perform.

On the contrary, they are inherent qualities that become a deep part of who you are and how you lead over time. They can't be stolen from you unless you let them go, and there is something about them that not only draws people to you but allows you to possess a deeper sense of confidence in your leadership. This is true because they bring a certain fullness and integrity to your life. You don't have to prove it, you just know it, and that's priceless knowledge for you as a leader.

> The core qualities to embrace are humility, gratitude, generosity, security, and courage.

The core qualities to embrace are humility, gratitude, generosity, security, and courage. There are a few more soul-level core qualities of a confident leader we could probably include, but for the purpose of this book, let's focus on these top five.

Embracing these qualities represents the last of the five deep foundational decisions. Before we jump into each one in more depth, let's return to Moses' narrative one last time. In it you will see just the tip of the iceberg of how these qualities are present within a leader's soul, and how they translate into life and confident leadership.

MOSES' HUMILITY

Even after seeing God work so vividly through Moses, Miriam and Aaron rose up against him, questioning whether he was truly God's chosen leader. "'Has the Lord spoken only through Moses?' they asked. 'Hasn't he also spoken through us?'" (Numbers 12:2). It's a much deeper hurt and hit to your confidence when doubt of and resistance to your leadership comes from those closest to you.

"Now Moses was a very humble man, more humble than anyone else on the face of the earth" (Numbers 12:3). That verse immediately follows the description of his siblings' rebellion for a very good reason: because ego was driving Miriam and Aaron. Yet, for Moses, humility was a marking quality or a part of his very core—apparently more so than anyone else on earth.

The Hebrew word for humility is *anav*, a concept that corresponds directly to passages like "the meek [humble] shall inherit the earth" (Psalm 37:11; Matthew 5:5). This *anav* humility was the secret of God's favor for Moses. As Psalm 147:6 says, "The LORD sustains the *anav* [humble]." And Isaiah 11:4 confirms God will decide with fairness for the *anav* of the earth.

Because humility was such a fundamental part of Moses' soul as a leader, his siblings were quickly exposed. God demanded to know how they dared speak against his chosen leader and cursed Miriam with leprosy. Her skin instantly turned white, and she was covered with sores.

Horrified by Miriam's disease, Aaron swiftly repented and begged Moses to intercede with God. Perhaps a proud man would have refused, but Moses was moved to forgive her. Then he humbly and graciously asked God to show her mercy by healing her.

The knowledge that, through humility, he had God's absolute favor had to be a supreme confidence builder for Moses. Humility was just one of the core qualities present in his life, and it gives us a clear picture of how our leadership is affected when, like Moses, our soul becomes aligned with God.

Inspirational Leadership

Moses lived to be 120 years old (Deuteronomy 34:7). God did not allow him to enter Canaan, but he did let him see Canaan with his own eyes (Deuteronomy 34:1–4). Moses, the one God knew face to face, died in Moab and was shown honor when God himself buried Moses there (Deuteronomy 34:5–6).

> Since then, no prophet has risen in Israel like Moses, whom the LORD knew face to face, who did all those signs and wonders the LORD sent him to do in Egypt—to Pharaoh and to all his officials and to his whole land. For no one has ever shown the mighty power or performed the awesome deeds that Moses did in the sight of all Israel. (Deuteronomy 34:10–12)

Studying his life inspires me personally to seek after these core qualities, beginning with embracing humility and aligning my leadership soul with God. After all, these qualities are not reserved uniquely for Moses. Let me tell you about my friend Sam.

A Conversation with Sam Chand

There are few people I respect and appreciate more than leadership architect and change strategist Sam Chand. When we spoke, I told him I saw all five core qualities in his life and asked him about his confidence as a leader. His answer was honest, humble, and full of gratitude.

Sam said, "Being a foreigner and an immigrant makes it very difficult to be confident. When you come to the United States on a student visa and experience the process of being naturalized with a green card, you are constantly second-guessing yourself. But I've always been grateful to be here."[1]

Sam moved from India to Atlanta, Georgia, in 1973 to become a Bible student at Beulah Heights Bible College. He graduated in 1977 and returned home to be the assistant pastor at his father's church for the next two years.

He then returned to Atlanta in 1979 and reconnected with Brenda, a close friend from college. They had a special spark and were married that same year.

What followed was a whirlwind of incredible experiences in church leadership. First, he was called to Oregon to serve as a youth pastor for two years, followed by a stint in Michigan as a senior pastor for nine years. Then, Beulah Heights Bible College in Atlanta called him to return, but this time, as its president. This was quite a stark contrast from his student days there when he worked as a janitor, breakfast cook, and even a dishwasher. Under his leadership, the school grew rapidly and is thriving today as Beulah Heights University. A number of well-known leaders took an interest in Sam, including John Maxwell, who asked him to head up Urban Leadership Development for the EQUIP organization while he was still serving as president at Beulah Heights.

Sam went on to share another insight about his confidence: "My confidence is 'borrowed' because it comes from the people I'm with. When I'm around confident leaders, I pick up their confidence. And when confident leaders believe in me, I gain confidence from that. At times I still hear the voice that says, 'You don't belong here. What are you doing here?' But my confidence comes from the fact that I was invited into the room."[2]

Sam Chand is one the smartest people I know, and I seek him out for coaching and counsel. He is always generous with his time and secure enough to speak hard truths to me, no matter what. I find that incredibly courageous.

Today, Sam is a sought-after and internationally acclaimed consultant, speaker, and bestselling author. Incidentally, he is also gratefully a citizen of the United States. It was a long road to get to this level of confidence as a leader, but he made it. And I'm convinced that it was due to the qualities in his soul as a leader.

Five Core Qualities to Embrace

1. Humility

Cultivating genuine humility in your life is a complex idea. For example, how much humility is enough? How does it fit in with confidence? Where do you start?

Humility isn't thinking poorly of yourself; it's thinking honestly about yourself. It's the combination of knowing the truth about yourself, and simultaneously understanding God's great love for you. When you see yourself and value yourself in the same way God does, you are headed in the right direction (Romans 12:3).

There is a paradox to humility, such as seen in Matthew 20:16: "So the last will be first, and the first will be last." Or consider Proverbs 22:4, which says, "Humility is the fear of the LORD; its wages are riches and honor and life." Or go one step further and look at James 4:10, "Humble yourselves before the Lord, and he will lift you up."

But while there is an element of paradox to humility, it is not a mystery. Humility is sometimes easier to see when compared to its opposite and evil brother, pride. Prideful leaders are arrogant, believe they are always right, can't say they are sorry, demand their own way, and often use people. On the contrary, humble leaders are kind, teachable, easy to be with, not demanding, lifters of others, have nothing to prove, and understand their gifts and abilities come from God.

> Humility isn't thinking poorly of yourself; it's thinking honestly about yourself.

Humility is not weakness; it is strength under control. It's a good balance of genuine self-awareness, God's gifts within you, and maturity. It does not diminish your leadership drive but increases your ability to lead from your most true self, which is always your most powerful self.

The power I'm referring to is the power of Christ working in you (Ephesians 3:20). The apostle Paul perhaps said it best: "For it is we who are the circumcision, we who serve God by his Spirit, who boast in Christ Jesus, and who put no confidence in the flesh—though I myself have reasons for such confidence. If someone else thinks they have reasons to put confidence in the flesh, I have more" (Philippians 3:3–4). A few short verses later, Paul provided balance to that statement by saying, "Not that I have already obtained all this, or have already arrived at my goal, but I press on to take hold of that for which Christ Jesus took hold of me" (Philippians 3:12).

Humility is best practiced and developed by seeking daily to be more like Christ. That is a lifelong endeavor for every leader who truly desires consistent and authentic confidence.

2. Gratitude

An ungrateful soul is an empty soul, because it always wants more. Some leaders are wired that way. Their insatiable drive for bigger and better can rob their souls of an essential quality of confident leaders: gratitude. When you lack gratitude, you lose confidence because something is always missing and you don't know what it is—but you know it's more of something. Perhaps it's a bigger church, a better staff, or faster growth.

I struggled for the longest time with Paul's teaching in Philippians 4:11–12, where he said he has learned to be content. I thought to myself, *I want to be content, but I'm not.* I'm always driving to the next goal, going after new territory, and pushing to extend our kingdom reach. It was easy for me to be grateful in my personal life, but as a leader, I wanted more. I wrestled because that drive always felt normal, healthy, and even God-designed. Then God gave me an insight to the difference between being content and being satisfied.

The desire within a leader to realize progress, to see the church grow and experience more lives changed, is normal and healthy. After all, that is God's purpose and plan. Lack of inner contentment comes, however, when God and I are out of sync. The problem is not my drive for new territory; it is when I think things should be bigger and move faster than God does. My part is to be in the game and give it 110 percent but then rest in the results, knowing I may be in charge but God is in control.

I can sum up this idea in one simple phrase: "I'm personally content but not leadership satisfied." Contentment is internal. Satisfaction is external. Nothing external brings lasting peace and contentment. It does not matter how big your church is, how many people are in small groups, or how many people are baptized, because leaders are never done. There is always one more person who needs God's love. Contentment comes from a quiet confidence that God is with me, he loves me, and I am living the life he has for me. From there, that contentment extends into my family life, leadership, and relationships with others. But it all starts from something deeply internal and personal with God.

If you possess personal inner contentment, then a mind-set of "never done and more to accomplish" is normal and good. Consider the opposite. You would never say, "Well, my church has reached enough people, and I'm fine with all our ministries as they are." There's not a chance you would think this because leaders lead. That inherently means you are eager to take new territory. However, if you lack personal contentment, never being satisfied can become your worst nightmare, because eventually, it will spill over into your family and church. You will attempt to get that missing contentment from them, or through them, rather than from God. When you and I are content in our relationship with Christ, meaning he is enough, then we are freed up to lead in a healthy and God-pleasing way. This gives us permission to not be satisfied with the current status of our churches and to press on to higher ground.

This will free you up to be a genuinely grateful leader. And when you are more joyful, people are drawn to you. You are naturally more grateful for all that you have, and you express gratitude to others easily and regularly.

3. Generosity

We often associate generosity with money, but that's a limited expression of a generous leader. Generosity runs deeper and broader as a core quality of a leader's soul. It's a way of living. It starts with humility, flows to gratitude, and naturally finds its way to generosity.

A generous leader not only shares with others financially but is generous with his or her time; expresses kind words of encouragement; opens doors of opportunity; is quick to offer help, wisdom, and good ideas; loves others sincerely; and leads for the benefit of others.

John Maxwell is one of the most generous leaders I know. It is just part of who he is. I was recently listening to him teach at a leadership conference, and he politely told the audience that he had to leave quickly to catch a flight as soon as he finished the last session. He normally stays till nearly the last person in the room leaves. Even after having made this announcement, about eight to ten people dashed up to the stage as soon as he finished speaking to ask questions or request a picture. I watched him graciously attend to each one while his staff was getting more antsy by the minute. Delta was not going to wait, not even for John. Finally, they whisked him away and he made his flight. His team would never tell me how fast they drove to get him to Hartsfield airport on time.

In addition to his effort to make time for the conference attendees,

I have personally experienced his generosity. After working together for twenty years, John and Margaret took Patti and me and longtime ministry partners and friends Tim Elmore and his wife, Pam, to London for a week to express his gratitude and love for all of us. It was a trip of a lifetime. To this day, we all still talk about those wonderful memories.

It was certainly an expression of incredible financial generosity. But many leaders might be tempted to think, *Well, if I were John Maxwell, I would do that too.* The point I want to make here is that John also did that kind of thing when he was the pastor of that little country church in Hillham, Indiana. It may not have been a trip to London, but he was equally generous for where he was at that stage of his life.

Here's the point: generosity is not dependent on how much money you make, it's a disposition of your soul. And again, it's about much more than money. It's a core quality confident leaders possess that permeates their whole lives. You can practice generosity daily by the words you speak, the love you give, the ideas you share, and the time you invest.

4. Security

I hope you can see that these core qualities build on each other. The soul qualities of humility, gratitude, and generosity naturally flow into being a secure leader. We discussed overcoming insecurity in chapter 2, and now let's add more depth by focusing on the disposition of a secure leader.

A sense of security is not merely the absence of insecurity. Inner peace, relative calm under pressure, and a nonanxious presence characterize the quality of a secure leader. There is a certain poise under fire that a secure leader possesses. They are comfortable in their own skin and not worried about what others think. The cumulative effect of these four qualities (humility, gratitude, generosity, and security) begin to exude tremendous confidence. It's not put on or worked up; it's the real you from the inside out. The people you lead will sense this quality within you. They will want to be a part of what you believe in and emulate these qualities themselves.

When it comes to vision, secure leaders don't have to sell. They inspire from what they believe. They know who they are and want what is best for others. Secure leaders may sometimes be in a hurry, but rarely are they in a panic or lead with a sense of chaos, even if things are on fire around them.

> Inner peace, relative calm under pressure, and a nonanxious presence characterize the quality of a secure leader.

A sense of personal security allows them to freely trust and empower, treat others with respect, make tough decisions, and share the credit. A secure nature helps prevent them from being guarded, protective, threatened, or fearful.

Embracing a genuine sense of security may be difficult if you don't first possess at least some humility, gratitude, and generosity within you. Remember, these are not skills to learn or competencies to perform; they represent a disposition of your heart and soul as a leader. And as I've mentioned, these core qualities are not a formula. They also are not always in order or equal in strength. But as you allow them to take hold in your life, your sense of confidence will rise dramatically and make way for the fifth quality: courage.

5. Courage

In many ways, courage is the sum of these first five chapters dealing with ownership, belief, identity, attentiveness, and soul. When you take ownership of your leadership confidence, believe in yourself and the fact that God is with you, know who you are and what you're called to do, walk closely with God and embrace these core qualities, courage is the anticipated outcome.

Confidence and courage go hand in hand, and they enable you as a leader to step up and do what needs to be done. Courage generally comes in two packages: the heroic type, such as a firefighter running into a blazing building to save a life, and the everyday kind that most of us tap into when we have to have a difficult conversation with someone. Both require guts and both are important. But it's typically the everyday courage that is needed in the majority of your church leadership. Everyday courage most commonly manifests itself in three expressions, and all require moral fiber:

- *Tough decisions.* Your leadership is determined and measured in large part by the decisions you make. You may only make five or ten truly tough decisions a year, but they mark your leadership and determine your future. The risk these tough decisions contain, and the courage required to do the right thing, will help shape your character.

- *Difficult conversations.* It's rare for a leader to enjoy confrontation, but all good leaders embrace rather than avoid those tough conversations. They take courage. You might be rejected, someone might leave the church, or a staff member might quit as a result, but you don't have an option if you want to lead well.
- *Public accountability.* Christian leaders, especially in the church, are held accountable for the way they live, in some respects more than any other profession. Anything less than sincere honesty and a moral life is grounds for dismissal, from personal integrity and family life to a public declaration of what we believe God is saying. That's the way it ought to be, but that kind of life requires resolve. It's not a life of perfection by any means, or none of us would qualify. But it does require courage.

It is my hope that these first five chapters and their corresponding deep foundational decisions help you prepare the way to more fully develop your character and more deeply build your confidence as a leader.

PART 2

DELIBERATE CHARACTER DEVELOPMENT

*Ability may get you to the top, but it
takes character to keep you there.*
—John Wooden

*If God should take his hands off my life, my lips
would turn to clay. I'm no great intellectual, and
there are thousands of men who are better preachers
than I am. You can't explain me if you leave out
the supernatural. I am but a tool of God.*[1]
—Billy Graham

Billy Graham (1918–2018) would be the first to say he didn't live a perfect life, and he would humbly confess that everything he accomplished was because of the grace of God. Perhaps that's part of why we all trusted him so much.

William Franklin Graham Jr. was born four days before World War I ended. Billy Frank, as his parents called him, grew up in modest surroundings on a dairy farm near Charlotte, North Carolina. He rose long before dawn to finish his chores before school. Of course, there was even more farmwork for him to do *after* school as well.[2] Needless to say, this industrious upbringing helped formed his character from a young age.

Billy loved baseball and hoped to play professionally, but in 1934, at sixteen years of age, he gave his life to Christ during a revival meeting led by evangelist Mordecai Ham.[3] This event would change the entire course of his life.

From his start as vice president of Youth for Christ (their first full-time employee) to an international crusade preacher, Reverend Graham spent his lifetime lifting up the name of Jesus. His spiritual authority and trusted character would eventually open unprecedented doors to the highest of places, including the White House. Amazingly, Graham became a spiritual advisor to all twelve presidents who held office during his ministry, regardless of political party, starting with Truman back in 1950, all the way up to President Obama.

Without a doubt, there must have been tremendous pressure on him from all sides to leverage his name or influence for political purposes, but Billy held his ground. He refused to campaign with candidates and always limited his guidance to be spiritual in nature.

Often called America's preacher, Billy Graham was known as one of the greatest evangelists of all time, but above all, he was known as a man of steadfast character. From his first sermon on Easter Sunday in 1937 at Bostwick Baptist Church (a small country church near Palatka, Florida)[4] to his last crusade in New York City in 2005, Billy was faithful in his consistent preaching of the gospel of Jesus Christ.

Over 58 years conducting 417 crusades in 185 countries, reaching 210 million people,[5] and during the 68 years since his first sermon, Billy Graham remained above reproach. This kind of integrity and brand of trustworthy character doesn't happen by accident. It involves a lifetime of deliberate and purposeful development.

The Billy Graham Rule

In 1948, Graham held a citywide evangelistic campaign in Modesto, California. Together with his team, consisting of Cliff Barrows, Grady

Wilson, and George Beverly Shea, they resolved "to avoid any situation that would have even the appearance of compromise or suspicion." Graham once said, "From that day on, I did not travel, meet, or eat alone with a woman other than my wife." This accountability agreement, later known as the Modesto Manifesto, covered not only their interactions with women, but also their commitments to integrity regarding how they handled finances, relationships with local churches, and publicity. It wasn't really a new lifestyle for them. "It did, however, settle in our hearts and minds once and for all, the determination that integrity would be the hallmark of both our lives and our ministry."[6]

They went public with their commitment, and to this day, it's a great example of sincere, resolute, and deliberate character development. The "rule" has received some criticism over the years, especially now in current culture, as being unnecessary or overly narrow. Nevertheless, thousands upon thousands of pastors have adopted it and proven it to be a wise choice.

Layering deliberate character development upon the deep foundational decisions described previously in part 1 is a powerful combination that will greatly strengthen your leadership confidence.

Next, as we dive into part 2, you will have the opportunity to work through five unique elements of your character that will significantly deepen your confidence as a leader: consistency, authority, adaptability, improvement, and resilience.

CHAPTER 6

CONSISTENCY

LEAD YOURSELF WELL BEFORE LEADING OTHERS

Primary greatness is on the inside. It's about character.
—STEPHEN COVEY

I had prayed a hopeful and perhaps overly ambitious prayer for ten years, asking God that I might have one minute with my spiritual hero, Dr. Billy Graham. That moment came on October 12, 1989.

John and Margaret Maxwell invited Patti and me to the fortieth anniversary celebration of Billy Graham's Evangelistic Crusades, sponsored by the Salvation Army. The time with John and Margaret was wonderful, and the dinner celebration honoring Dr. Graham was amazing. But a private moment with Billy Graham was, to a young pastor, a once-in-a-lifetime gift.

The evening was fast paced, and there were probably fifty to seventy-five reporters pressing in on the famous seventy-one-year-old evangelist before the celebration started. Somehow in all the hustle and commotion, John, Dr. Graham, and I ended up in a private room for several minutes together.

Here's what struck me at that moment. I was a "kid" pastor, not known to anyone, and Dr. Graham treated me as if I was the most important person in the world. After talking with John, he then fully focused on me. Very kindly, he asked a couple of questions about what I did at the church. He looked me in the eyes the whole time and called me by name as we left.

The impact has never left me. Dr. Graham was the same in private as he was in public. He was a man of character—a man of God. That strong consistency of life and leadership adds confidence to any leader because possessing a depth of integrity is something you can trust.

The People You Lead Count on You

Self-leadership is the essence of character development. You can't lead others well until you can lead yourself well. And leading yourself can't be a full-time job. You've met leaders like that, right? They just seem to have trouble getting their act together. We all have stuff to work on, but there's a big difference between leaders who are continually growing and leaders who seem to get stuck and circle the same issues over and over again.

> Self-leadership is the essence of character development.

It might be things that are seemingly benign, such as being consistently late for meetings or not following through on small tasks like returning phone calls or responding to emails. Basically, it comes down to not doing what they said they'd do. It can also escalate to things like rollercoaster emotions, a need for control, or even abusing authority.

The people who attend your church are not looking for a superhero to lead them; they're looking for someone they can count on. They want a leader who can consistently show up and do the right thing. The expectation is not one of a perfect leader but a leader whose self-leadership is worth following.

David: The Passionate Leader

When King Saul was tormented by an evil spirit, he sent his attendants to find someone to provide him comfort through music (1 Samuel 16:14–17). He was soon told that a man from Bethlehem named Jesse had a young son, David, who could help. The report they gave of the boy was glowing (1 Samuel 16:18):

- He is a skillful musician.
- He is a brave warrior.
- He is handsome and speaks well.
- The LORD is with him.

David quickly found favor with Saul and became one of his armor bearers (1 Samuel 16:21–22). As time went on, David's responsibilities and prominence continued to grow until he eventually became king himself.

David, like Moses, was a great leader. He possessed a passionate love for God and was loved by the people. The overall picture of his life reveals a character you could count on, but it also tells us about the inescapable consequences resulting from a lack of consistency.

A break in consistency of doing the right thing will always hurt your confidence as a leader. You can come back, like David did, but there will be consequences. Accordingly, the more consistent you are in your character, the more confident you will become as a leader.

We will explore a recounting of David's story across these next five chapters, beginning with a narrative that demonstrates the significance of consistency. Part of what made David great was not the absence of sin but that he possessed the character to own his sin. David was repentant at a heart level and continued to sincerely chase after God.

DAVID'S BREAK IN CONSISTENCY

It is well known that Scripture calls David a man "after God's own heart," an incredible title given to no other (1 Samuel 13:14; Acts 13:22).

When David was young, God took the throne of Israel away from the faithless King Saul and replaced him with David. God even honored David with the privilege of having the Messiah descend from his line. Why?

David had a unique passion for God and reverence for his Word (Psalm 19:7–14; 2 Samuel 7:18–24). Challenge after challenge, even when his life was at stake, David consistently refused to compromise and showed a deep determination to follow God well, no matter the cost.

This forged a continual strength of character in him that God could rely on, which in turn, formed great confidence in David. Ironically, when David was established, it was because of this confidence that he relaxed and weakness crept in.

"In the spring, at the time when kings go off to war . . . David remained in Jerusalem" (2 Samuel 11:1). David could have done what he had always done: lead his army to victory. But instead, he stayed home. For the first time, his private behavior diverged from his public persona.

While his men were in a distant land fighting on his behalf, David strolled on the roof of his palace looking down in lust upon one of the most beautiful women he'd ever seen as she bathed—a violation of God's law. And worse, Bathsheba was the beloved wife of one of his top military officers, Uriah the Hittite.

David's early years were marked by a willingness to sacrifice himself for his men. Now David not only put his friend and servant's life at risk in war without the benefit of his leadership, but he was nurturing lustful thoughts about the servant's wife while he was away.

This inconsistency formed a weakness in David. It was a weakness like a brittle spot in an oak tree or an unseen crack in the blade of a sword. These were flaws that allow a shattering when pressed. Tragically, David let himself to fall into adultery with Bathsheba. Then, if that were not enough betrayal, he even arranged to have Uriah murdered on the front lines of battle to cover it up.

This didn't just hurt David; it grieved the heart of God.

The betrayal and adultery followed by murder would wreak devastating consequences on David's life. He would soon learn just how much inconsistency costs. And among those costs would be a great deal of lost confidence.

Character over Competence

I'll admit my hesitance to place character over competence, because they're both vitally important. And candidly, I'm type A and driven enough to lean in to my skills and determination to get things done. We have to be good at what we do and continue to improve, which we'll talk about more in chapter 8. Competence and character are a partnership that should be inseparable, but unfortunately, they're not.

The bottom line is that a lack of competence can slow you down, but a lack of character can take you out. If you lack skill, you can improve; if you lack character, you are destined for a fall. Character isn't measured in a linear fashion, but in some ways, the greater the lack of character, the greater the fall. You may not be permanently out of ministry from a breach in character, but the road back can be long and difficult.

There are stories of a one-time lapse in an otherwise stellar character, but those stories are unusual; typically, there has been something brewing underneath for some time. For example, of the leaders who have told me their stories of marital affairs, not one said he woke up one morning and decided, "I think I'll wreck my life today." Not one guy who was in love with his wife, doing well at his church, and walking with God did that.

> A lack of competence can slow you down, but a lack of character can take you out.

Unhappy at home and stressed at work, they first flirted with the idea, then tested temptation, and slowly gave in. That's a more common path to a breakdown in character. It doesn't matter what the circumstance may be—whether it's about money, sex, or power—that's the path. And sadly, a leader's confidence follows down that path of destruction right along with character.

The Secret Is in Consistency

One of the least discussed developmental essentials to a strong character is consistency. Unfortunately, consistency is often thought of as boring, inflexible, or lacking creativity. It, however, is not meant to reflect a lack of drive, unwillingness to risk, or stirring things up when needed. Consistency is a core character trait, not a measurement of competence.

Consistency is about keeping your promises and doing what you say you will do. That's character. Consistency allows people to approach you, not because your emotions are flat, but because you are a safe person to talk to and you can be counted on. Consistency is a primary avenue to trust.

A young student pastor asked to see me for coffee. He told me the story about a major conflict he had with his boss that led to him being fired. His boss, the senior pastor, was gifted, charismatic, and a hard worker. He had a fiery personality that made for great preaching and vision casting but that also produced confusion and hurt in private meetings. He was very inconsistent. One day he would be up and positive, and the next day he would be down, seemingly angry about everything. Finally, the young pastor confronted his boss, but it was apparently on the wrong day and he was fired on the spot.

Developing consistency to strengthen your character requires self-leadership. No one can do this for you. Consistency can best be developed in three areas: your habits, your emotions, and your words. These three combined are powerful allies to increase your confidence as a leader. As I mentioned earlier, when you can first count on and trust yourself, there is simply no price tag you can place on what that does for you and your leadership.

Self-awareness and self-leadership are directly connected. As we discussed in chapter 3, the process begins with you first becoming increasingly self-aware. That enables you to self-manage, or self-lead. Now let's look at the three important areas to focus on.

1. Your Habits

It's sobering how only a few bad habits can overshadow a dozen or more good habits. For example, overall, I eat healthy (except on my birthday when I eat chocolate chip cookies until I quietly slip into a sugar coma), exercise regularly, see my doctor for regular checkups, work on reducing unnecessary stress, drink lots of water, and avoid sugar. These are all good habits. However, I struggle with eating later at night than I should. In terms of my health, that one bad habit wreaks havoc on all my good habits. No one can fix this but me. It's up to my self-leadership to change this bad habit to a good habit of not eating at least three hours before I go to bed. And consistency is key. It doesn't help much if I'm successful once a week. My habit needs consistency to be effective.

The same principle is in play specifically within the realm of leadership. The majority of your time should be invested in developing good leadership habits. But if you ignore the few bad habits you have, they can nearly erase the good ones. Further, persistent bad habits decrease your effectiveness because they erode your leadership confidence.

You probably know your bad habits. I know mine. They're different for everyone. Some bad habits are seemingly harmless but can still reflect on your character. For example, anything from frequently canceling meetings to micromanaging others may seem like small indiscretions. Others, however, are more serious and the potential list of detriments is long. These may include using grace to avoid tough conversations, allowing guilt to misdirect your time and energy, letting busyness overtake productivity, overplaying your authority to win a decision, or giving in to comparing and complaining. It doesn't take much of any of these bad habits, or those like them, to neutralize many of your good habits.

> It's sobering how only a few bad habits can overshadow a dozen or more good habits.

It's possible, too, that you don't see your bad habits. If you're not sure what they are, ask a friend or colleague to be honest with you. As we discussed in part 1, being vulnerable by allowing others the space and permission to speak frankly with you will build your confidence. If you learn something you didn't know, that's a great gift to you. Once you know, the next step is to own it. Take responsibility and make a plan of action. If conquering it on your own is not possible, such as with any number of addictions, seek some professional help and accountability. Don't waste your talent, crash your confidence, and maybe lose your ministry. Ask for help.

2. Your Emotions

As a leader, you experience the full array of human emotions on a regular basis. How you handle your emotions can make or break your leadership.

Jesus, too, experienced a full range of emotions, including love, anger, compassion, loneliness, frustration, and joy. The powerful thing about Jesus and the expression of his emotions, however, is that it always seemed to be perfectly appropriate and perfectly timed. Each of his expressions was consistent and appropriate to the moment. But let's be honest, we're not Jesus. We are called to live like him, but we'll never be him, so self-leadership is vital. Here are three ways to take control of your emotions:

- *Own your emotions.* Never blame your emotions on your circumstances or other people. For example, it's easy to think that a particular person made you angry. When I'm in rush-hour traffic moving at a snail's pace on Interstate 85 in Atlanta, and someone blasts their horn at me as if I could go faster, I don't immediately think "Jesus thoughts."

  It's true that someone can push your buttons, provoke you, and cause an emotion like anger to begin to rise up within you. But it is your emotion, and you choose how you will respond. If it were true that someone could actually make you angry, that would mean they could control you. Even in traffic.

  The same is true with gratitude, happiness, and contentment, for example. No one can make you feel grateful, happy, or content. These are choices you make. If other people were responsible for your happiness, you could only experience as much happiness as they could or would give you, and we know that's not true. Being in control of your emotions does not suggest a robotlike personality. Rather, it's an indication of mature and spirit-filled leadership.

- *Lead your emotions.* Either you lead your emotions, or they lead you. While leading your emotions is not always easy to do, it's vitally important for a leader. When you're under pressure, stressed, tired, or feeling overwhelmed, that's when it is most crucial. It is about being aware of and present with your feelings. This enables you to guide and shape them, rather than being owned or controlled by them.

  Let's take positive emotions as an example. Your work as a spiritual leader is serious work. It involves people, problems, and even spiritual warfare. Over time, this process will drain you. Therefore, it's necessary for you to purposely cultivate positive emotions, such as joy, gratitude, love, compassion, and contentment. You can choose to laugh, play, serve, and give. You can choose staff, friends, and even service providers you enjoy being around. You can take charge and lead your emotions, rather than be governed by them. That's what self-leadership looks like.

- *Mature your emotions.* Maturing your emotions is the goal of owning and leading your emotions. No one wants to live like a machine or expects you to have perfectly contained emotions. Your emotions are an expression of life and make you an interesting person. At the same time, people can't trust a leader whose emotions are unpredictable and may erupt at any moment. Active volcanos are only fun from a distance!

> Either you lead your emotions, or they lead you.

Remaining poised when the heat is on is an indication of maturity. And emotional maturity needs to be free and real, and at the same time, self-controlled and even-tempered. Prayer, wise counsel, and intentional effort, combined with selfless living, are key components that help your emotions mature.

There are three emotions that can take you out. They can be positive motivators or negative paralyzers. For example, fear can cause you to get out of the way of an oncoming car, and anger can be appropriately expressed against injustice. But for the context of this chapter, I'll focus on the need to wisely learn to own, lead, and mature these emotions in a consistently appropriate manner.

- *Fear.* Fear paralyzes a leader and robs him or her of confidence. It can prevent a leader from doing a host of important things, such as taking a risk, having a tough conversation, or even being obedient to a prompt of God. Fear of failure, looking foolish, or disappointing someone can even cause a leader to hold back from doing the right thing.

I briefly mentioned in chapter 2 that one of the best antidotes to fear is action. If you are struggling with fear, try this helpful exercise: break each fear-producing situation down to bite-size pieces and tackle it one piece at a time.

A friend of mine has some health-related fears. He is overly concerned with what *might* be wrong with him. When I encouraged him to take one bite-size step to see a doctor, he was reluctant for fear of what he might discover. However, that's exactly what he should do to either alleviate the fear or face it and conquer it. Resist the temptation to make a decision aligned with fear, rather than faith.

- *Anger.* Unmanaged anger is a true nemesis to even the best of leaders. One ill-timed blowup can cost much. Depending on the severity of the circumstance or the public nature of an outburst, it can even cost a leader his or her leadership. The good news is that for one instance, there is usually enough grace for it to be relatively easily repaired, especially if accompanied by openness and humility.

  If you struggle with anger, however, or if it's a pattern in your life, I would encourage you to seek out a wise and experienced counselor to get underneath the anger and discover its origin. I've heard it said that anger is actually a secondary emotion fueled by hurt or pain. You don't need to remain captive to the fallout of unresolved issues from your past. Freedom from anger is within reach, but you can't obtain it by yourself. Talk with a trusted friend or counselor soon.

- *Discouragement.* Discouragement is one of the top tactics used by the Devil to take spiritual leaders out. It's not enough to disqualify a leader like anger can, and it doesn't completely shut down a leader like fear can, but it's enough to distract a leader from being his or her best. And over the long haul, that can have a huge effect on the leader's confidence.

  Discouragement often originates from a lie based on skewed perspective. For example, your church attendance may have been down last week, but you had a good number of visitors, several people were saved, and the offering was strong. The Enemy wants you to focus on the things that didn't go right, like the low attendance, because all the other factors will encourage you, which will motivate you to keep going.

> **Fear paralyzes a leader and robs him or her of confidence.**

Overcoming discouragement can most often be achieved by spending some time with a few positive-natured, hopeful, and trusted leaders who believe in you and see the good that is happening. It's also important that you don't allow yourself to become or remain isolated from others. Isolation is one of the most common behaviors sure to move your perspective off center.

3. Your Words

Your words reflect your heart (Luke 6:45). This means, among the key habits of the heart, the words you speak reflect your character second only to your actions or habits. Anyone can be on their best behavior for a couple of hours or a couple of days, but eventually, their words will expose them for who they really are on the inside.

> **Your words reflect your heart.**

David himself understood how difficult it is to consistently speak uplifting words. You can see this reflected in these two passages David wrote in the Psalms:

> Set a guard over my mouth, LORD;
> keep watch over the door of my lips.
> Do not let my heart be drawn to what is evil
> so that I take part in wicked deeds
> along with those who are evildoers;
> do not let me eat their delicacies.
>
> (PSALM 141:3–4)

> May these words of my mouth and this meditation of my heart
> be pleasing in your sight,
> LORD, my Rock and my Redeemer.
>
> (PSALM 19:14)

The following three attributes of the heart are expressed through your words:

- *Honesty.* The people you lead depend on your honesty. Your truthfulness is the basis of their trust in you, and honesty is foundational to your character. No matter how great the temptation is to exaggerate, back off when confrontation is needed, or even spin something to your advantage, you should choose complete honesty.
- *Hope.* The people you lead know that life can be difficult, so they need hope for a better future. As a leader, you not only speak words of hope, but you demonstrate that hope by the vision you cast, decisions you make, and words you speak in day-to-day conversations. We will address this topic further in chapter 14.
- *Honor.* Speaking words that build others up, communicate value, and show respect are invaluable to you as a leader. However, without sincerity, even these beautiful words can ring hollow. But when spoken from the heart, the impact is deep, meaningful, and lasting.

Self-leadership is needed to maintain productive habits, positive emotions, and uplifting words. The more consistently you live these out, the more your confidence as a leader grows.

This becomes the foundation on which you can carry the authority given to you, which is the subject of our next chapter.

CHAPTER 7

AUTHORITY

ACCEPT IT, DEVELOP IT, AND USE IT WISELY

*Nearly all men can stand adversity, but if you
want to test a man's character, give him power.*
—ABRAHAM LINCOLN

Every sophomore at my high school feared the name of one DMV officer at the La Mesa, California, branch of the department of motor vehicles. He was notorious for failing students attempting to get their driver's licenses. This was decades ago, yet I remember it like it was yesterday.

As I stood in line waiting, I was excited to gain the independence that comes with a driver's license and scared to death that I might get "him." It was my turn. They called my name, and I walked outside only to see "him" standing by my car. My heart sank.

I was really nervous. I tried to be nice to him. I *had* to be nice to him. This guy had the authority to grant my freedom or keep it from me. I started the car and did everything according to my training. I remembered to fasten my seatbelt, adjust the mirrors correctly, and then, looking both ways, I headed toward the parking lot exit.

We pulled up to the intersection and he said, "Turn left." *Okay*, I thought, *easy enough*. This was a simple and relatively quiet residential-size two-way street. I put my blinker on and waited because traffic was coming into the lane I needed to drive in. He said again, "Turn left." But this time a little louder. I didn't go because cars were still coming. It was an unusually busy time. Then for the third time, and in a loud and irritated voice, he said, "Turn left!"

I replied, "I can't. Cars are coming."

He yelled, "Go now!"

I whipped out into the wrong lane and slowly drove down the wrong side of the street for about twenty-five feet. I was heading into what could have been oncoming traffic had there been a car there in that moment.

Immediately, he growled, "Pull over!"

I obeyed and pulled over to the side of the road. He wrote a big red *F* on my exam paper and said, "You're done." When I asked why, he replied, "You were driving on the wrong side of the street!" I was dumbfounded, and without mercy he seemed to enjoy the moment.

Perhaps you, too, have encountered someone who has misused their authority in some way. Maybe it was a professor, a boss, a police officer, a business partner, or even a leader in the church. When someone does this, it always reflects poorly on their character. For some, of course, it could be a one-time thing. After all, everyone has a bad day on occasion. What I'm referring to is a consistent pattern that is also recognized by others, not only you.

Authority, Influence, and Power

As a leader, you can never escape the reality of authority and its reflection on your character. "There is a currency through which leaders get things done. It's called authority. Some people prefer to use the term *influence*, and that word does more accurately describe the innate function of leadership."[1] If you can't handle authority, you will struggle with leadership, and your confidence may be challenged because of the pressure you face.

> If you can't handle authority, you will struggle with leadership.

Perhaps a helpful way to see how these

84

leadership concepts interact is to compare three closely related words: *authority, influence,* and *power.*

- Authority is something given to you.
- Influence is what you possess within you.
- Power is your ability to cause good or harm.

All three words are intricately connected, and understanding how they're related will allow you to use them somewhat interchangeably, while focusing more so on the concept of authority.

Let's return to the story of David and see how one demonstration of authority is connected to confidence.

DAVID AND GOD'S AUTHORITY

Long before David met Bathsheba, he was an unassuming youth who knew nothing of the world beyond the sheep he tended daily and the wisdom he learned sitting at his father's feet.

While David's brothers were away from home fighting the Philistines as a part of Saul's army, his parents kept him home with the flocks. He was the youngest and probably no more than fifteen years old. Some scholars believe his name in Hebrew could have meant "beloved or cared for," so the idea that this untested youth could become the savior of Israel would have been inconceivable to most.

The reason for the war was a yearning for freedom. The Philistines were vicious oppressors of the Israelites for centuries, and Saul was the first leader with the gall to stand up to them by raising an army to break the bondage.

Yet, as the Israelite army faced the Philistines across the Valley of Elah, Saul held back in fear along with his men. For more than a month, a giant of a man named Goliath had come out to challenge the Israelites every morning and afternoon.

The challenge from the Philistines was simple: send your best warrior to fight Goliath. This was not going to be easy, and the stakes were high because the losing side would serve the other as slaves.

Goliath stood over nine feet tall and had the muscle and strength to match. A lack of confidence had created this standoff. For forty days, no Israelite dared try. The risk of losing was too great.

Early one morning, David's father sent him on a journey to bring his brothers some supplies. Upon seeing their little brother, however, his older siblings had nothing but ridicule. "Why have you come down here? And with whom did you leave those few sheep in the wilderness? I know how conceited you are . . . you came down only to watch the battle," the eldest brother said (1 Samuel 17:28).

But David heard Goliath's words: "This day I defy the armies of Israel!" And something sparked within. David soon found himself on the battlefield, armed with nothing but a sling, five smooth stones, and courage.

"David said to the Philistine, 'You come against me with sword and spear and javelin, but I come against you in the name of the Lord Almighty, the God of the armies of Israel, whom you have defied'" (1 Samuel 17:45).

David's great confidence came directly from a sense of authority derived from God. He believed that since the armies of Israel belonged to God, to defy them was to defy God himself. And he knew God would defend his own name.

This understanding of authority is what gave David his confidence while all others trembled. The result was one dead giant and a group of people freed.

Authority and Confidence

Your level of confidence can cause you to overplay or underplay your authority. Some leaders misunderstand their authority, become overconfident, and therefore misuse it. Others back away from their authority, lacking the confidence to carry out their responsibilities. Which direction do you lean?

The interaction of authority and confidence within you can greatly determine how well you develop your influence. Your influence is always either slowly increasing or decreasing; it never remains the same, any more than your life circumstances. It may seem like it's steady, but that's only because the local church operates in a highly relational manner and therefore often moves slowly. But don't mistake slow for secure and guaranteed.

Far too many leaders get blindsided by this issue. They tell me their stories and they usually start with something like, "I thought everything was fine. We were all doing great together. Then, all of a sudden, the wheels came off."

> Your influence is always either slowly increasing or decreasing; it never remains the same.

I may not know all the details, but I can promise you the wheels didn't fall apart all of a sudden. It was happening for a long time, but they didn't see it. Their influence was decreasing, perhaps ever so slowly, and slipping away. These situations obviously have a big effect on a leader's confidence.

The good news is, the path to increasing your influence is not a mystery. If you've not read John Maxwell's book *The 5 Levels of Leadership*, I highly recommend you do so at your earliest opportunity. For now, let me offer you a number of ways you can know that your influence is increasing:

- More people seek you out.
- People say yes easier and faster.
- People's loyalty toward you increases.
- More people want to know what you think.
- You are trusted with greater levels of responsibility.
- People's trust in you as a person increases.
- Your productivity increases.
- People follow your vision with greater enthusiasm.
- Favor and momentum are not strangers to you.
- You get promoted.
- More people want to be on your team.

When your character is true and your influence is increasing, God is then able to extend your authority to a greater extent, much like he did for Jo Anne.

A Conversation with Jo Anne Lyon

Jo Anne Lyon, the extraordinary founder of World Hope International, started life as the down-to-earth daughter of humble church planters. Born in Blackwell, Oklahoma, her parents were pioneers and leaders, hosting tent revival meetings and founding churches. Those they brought to Christ would become the core for a new church plant, and every three to four years, they were able to hand off an established church to another pastor. Then it was off to plant another church.

Together, her family planted fourteen churches in all. This was the environment Jo Anne grew up in and how she gained much of her entrepreneurial and leadership spirit.

She started a teaching career in urban Cincinnati, Ohio, but after seven years giving of herself to students in a classroom, she decided to invest the next decade of her life leading federally funded inner-city programs that worked to fight poverty and improve education in Kansas City, Missouri.

In 1996, feeling determined to tackle big issues such as poverty, justice, and bringing hope to the marginalized, Jo Anne founded World Hope International. I asked her how she would describe her confidence as a leader. Her response? "Much of my early confidence came from being affirmed by others. Being a female leader, I was never sure I belonged, especially in church circles. But as God began to confirm my leadership, particularly in founding and leading World Hope, my confidence began to grow."[2]

Over the years, God continued to grow her authority. In 2008, she became the General Superintendent of the Wesleyan Church, and eventually its Ambassador/General Superintendent Emeritus.

I've known Jo Anne for a long time. Through her long and varied career, there has never been a break in her standards. Even in the midst of the uniqueness of relationships in Washington, DC, where World Hope is based, she has not wavered from her faith or convictions.

When I asked Jo Anne about how she related to authority as a leader, she said, "I rarely thought about authority. My mind and heart were always focused on the heaviness of responsibility."[3] It was never about power for Jo Anne, it was about purpose. She was much like David in his battle with Goliath in that what drove him was a sense of responsibility to exert

God-given authority for the sake of defending God's honor. It was not a power grab. Jo Anne handled authority with humility.

In 2005, Jo Anne and I were part of a team that traveled to Sri Lanka right after a terrible tsunami in hopes of bringing help and relief to people who were suffering. I remember sitting in a meeting with a representative from the Sri Lankan government and listening to a conversation between a certain government official and Jo Anne, both of whom had tremendous authority and were decision makers.

They had never met previously, but I could tell he trusted her. I believe it was because he knew she cared, wanted to help in the midst of a crisis, and didn't care that they were Buddhists. She wasn't there to deliver a pre-packaged program but to ask him, "What do you need?"

Her use of authority representing World Hope, the Wesleyan Church, and, candidly, global Christianity, was pure and for good. There was no agenda except to help. And God continues to honor that motive to this day. Spiritual authority used correctly is kingdom oriented, not based on human gain. This kind of authority is used to serve for the good of others, and it is intricately connected to increased confidence because you know the ultimate source is God.

Three Myths About Leadership Authority

1. Your Authority in the Organization Determines Your Influence

Clay Scroggins, the lead pastor at Buckhead Church, North Point Ministries, said, "Life teaches us that the authority to lead and the opportunity to lead are a package deal. We think that they go hand in hand like cranberry sauce and turkey. When we're given the authority to lead—a title, a uniform, a corner office—then, and only then, we will have the opportunity to lead. But that's just not true."[4]

Clay's right. Your level of influence is not governed by your level of authority. When

> Your confidence will rise when you know it's *you* they listen to, not your title.

you can emotionally let go of your title and your spot on the organization chart, you discover real influence. And in contrast, if you attempt to demand, command, or force your authority, you decrease your influence. The real leaders always rise. If you want to know who the real leader is at the table, pay attention to the person everyone looks to for their opinion, approval, or decision. Your confidence will rise when you know it's *you* they listen to, not your title.

2. Your Authority Is Independent from Your Character

You have undoubtedly met leaders you didn't trust. It might have been based on a personal experience or a gut feeling. Regardless, if asked about them, you would not give a positive endorsement. And yet they still have positions in their organizations. This can make it appear like authority and character are independent from each other, but authority and character are always connected. It may take time and usually requires pressure, but eventually, either a respectable or regrettable character emerges.

3. Your Level of Authority Determines Your Level of Confidence

Only an inexperienced leader believes that the higher they rise in the organization, the more their confidence increases. That leader thinks, *When I'm in charge, I'll be able to make the decisions and make things happen.* They are destined for an unfortunate but insightful awakening. In fact, the moment real conflict, competing priorities, and pressure hits, their confidence shrinks, because they assumed their title would carry them through and it never does. It happens innocently. You get promoted because someone sees potential in you, and your confidence rises. That's good. But your confidence is borrowed until you prove your leadership in your new position by what you actually accomplish.

Authority Is Always Transferred

The transition of Moses' leadership to Joshua gives us great insight about authority:

> The LORD said to Moses, "Take Joshua son of Nun, a man in whom is the spirit of leadership, and lay your hand on him. Have him stand before

Eleazar the priest and the entire assembly and commission him in their presence. Give him some of your authority so the whole Israelite community will obey him. He is to stand before Eleazar the priest, who will obtain decisions for him by inquiring of the Urim before the LORD. At his command he and the entire community of the Israelites will go out, and at his command they will come in." (Numbers 27:18–21)

Moses is literally instructed by God to give Joshua some of his authority (v. 20). You can clearly see the close connection between natural influence and spiritual authority ("spirit of leadership" in verse 18) and formal authority ("so the whole Israelite community will obey him" in verse 20). All this is connected in the transfer of authority from Moses to Joshua.

The authority you have has been transferred to you as well. The amount of authority you have been given is an indication of the level of trust those above you have placed in you. This process starts with the source of authority. As I wrote in my book *Amplified Leadership*, "There are two primary sources of authority: God and man. In ministry, the two are intricately connected. Ultimately, God is the source of a spiritual leader's authority, but if our understanding of authority stops there, we could easily become answerable to no one."[5]

The important distinction is that you are never the source of your own authority. That core principle has significant impact on the development of your character as well as confidence. When you understand that your leadership authority doesn't belong to you but has been entrusted to you, you carry it differently. You are more likely to steward it with wisdom, grace, and strength of character. The complication, however, is that as the leader you are still held responsible.

> You are never the source of your own authority.

When I passed my driver's test the second time I took it, the state of California transferred their authority to me in the form of a driver's license so I could legally drive a car. But I was still held responsible to obey and respect the rules of the road or my license could be revoked. If the license was actually mine, it could not be taken away from me.

When I was ordained as a Wesleyan pastor, formal and spiritual authority was transferred to me by denominational officials. A great trust was placed in me, and my confidence was strengthened. Every year, however, my leadership is evaluated, and, depending on the assessment, my licensing may be renewed or revoked. How I handle my authority determines the outcome.

Jesus always referred to his authority in direct relationship to the Father. In fact, he stated that he does nothing apart from the Father (John 5:19; John 8:28). A dozen Scripture passages referring to the transference of authority are listed in the endnotes for this chapter,[6] but here are three for quick reference:

1. Jesus' authority was transferred from the Father.
   "For as the Father has life in himself, so he has granted the Son also to have life in himself. And he has given him authority to judge because he is the Son of Man." (John 5:26–27)

2. Jesus transferred his authority to the disciples.
   When Jesus had called the Twelve together, he gave them power and authority to drive out all demons and to cure diseases, and he sent them out to proclaim the kingdom of God and to heal the sick. (Luke 9:1–2)

3. Jesus' authority transferred to all believers.
   Then Jesus came to them and said, "All authority in heaven and on earth has been given to me. Therefore go and make disciples of all nations, baptizing them in the name of the Father and of the Son and of the Holy Spirit, and teaching them to obey everything I have commanded you. And surely I am with you always, to the very end of the age." (Matthew 28:18–20)

Regardless of the amount of authority you have been given or whether you are the senior pastor or a volunteer leader in the church, ask yourself if you lead in such a way as to honor the one who trusted you with the authority.

You are empowered to lead, yet at the same time, you are responsible to follow. Another key question is, Are you willing to remain under authority, or to submit, to the person who is the source of your authority? This test is not always passed with flying colors. Even Jesus' disciples argued among themselves about who would be greatest. And Jesus had to teach them again about authority (Luke 22:24–27).

Let's be honest. No one likes being told what to do. Right? After more than thirty years of marriage, I can still resist my wife Patti's authority to tell me to put the toilet seat down, whether it's done in an uplifting and inspiring way or in the form of a strong request with expectations of changed behavior.

We can bristle under authority or flat-out resist it. When this occurs in your heart as a leader, it reveals that you forgot where your authority came from and is possibly a reflection of something within you that needs to be resolved. When submission is no longer freely demonstrated, authority is usually mishandled.

For a long time, King Saul wrongly persecuted David for suspected treason, of which David was completely innocent. This persecution meant that David literally had to flee for his life from Saul's army and live in the wilderness for years, wondering every day if that one would be his last. Even worse, all this happened *after* the most revered religious leader in the land, the prophet Samuel, had anointed David with holy oil and appointed him to be the next king, thus proclaiming God was taking the kingdom away from Saul.

What man has ever had a better excuse to buck authority? Doing so would not only save his life but fulfill a prophecy. Yet, when Saul was most vulnerable in a cave and David could have easily ended the failed king's life, he refused. Instead, David chose to remain under the authority of the "Lord's anointed" (1 Samuel 24:6), even if it meant continuing to live under the risk of dying. To him, to respect Saul's authority was to respect the authority of God himself, and it was up to God to remove it.

Your leadership must always come under authority, and this is best accomplished by acknowledging the source of your authority. Further, the authority that has been transferred to you is solely for the purpose of accomplishing the mission and for the good of the people.

Authority from the Other Side of the Desk

A senior pastor said it well in one sentence: "I never truly understood authority until I sat on the other side of the desk." He shared the story about all the years he was on staff as a pastor in various positions. He was honest about resisting what his boss, the senior pastor, asked of him, always wanting to do things his way, and using his influence to get what he wanted. He told me about how one time the pastor gave him global missions to lead, but a couple of years later when the pastor wanted to move global missions to another staff member, he resisted, saying, "It's my ministry, I built it."

He simply forgot who gave it to him in the first place. Now that he led his own staff, the issue of authority and how it works has become much clearer. This includes the authority from above him that was extended to him by the church board. I found it insightful when he said his leadership confidence was now actually stronger because he isn't fighting to possess and gain more authority, but merely stewarding what he has been given.

As you learn to embrace and handle your authority in a way that pleases God and serves your church well, your confidence will rise and free you from issues like ownership and control. You can then focus on adaptability and the ability to change—the subject of the next chapter.

CHAPTER 8

ADAPTABILITY

LOOK FOR WAYS TO BECOME THE
BEST VERSION OF YOU

*Embrace uncertainty. Some of the most beautiful chapters
in our lives won't have a title until much later.*
—Bob Goff

Moving from San Diego to Atlanta was a huge change that required my family and me to adapt to a different culture, geography, weather, and to the millions of loud bugs called cicadas. Having been born and raised in San Diego, and then raising our family there, it was home for all of us. It was our life, and I didn't want to leave. When you're about to trade the Pacific Ocean for the Chattahoochee River, you instinctively think, this can't be what God has in mind. It's easy to begin second-guessing yourself and wonder if it's the right thing to do, which then chips away at your confidence to make it happen.

We made the move and gratefully it didn't take long before we met great people and started making new friends. God was also adding favor to our ministry. But we still felt unsettled. God seemed to be telling us to "trust me in this." We then soon discovered something that made us feel more at home: Lake Lanier. The site of the 1996 Olympics, it's a beautiful lake that covers 59 square miles of water and 692 miles of shoreline, and our kids loved boating all over it.

I didn't have to make this move, so why did I? First, God clearly called me to something new. Knowing that God was with me provided life-giving confidence. Second, it continued my ministry partnership with John Maxwell. And third, I knew that if I had stayed in San Diego, I would have become comfortable and possibly stopped growing. That's not true for everyone, but in my case it was. I needed to change and adapt to a new way of life.

Looking back, it's easy to see what God was up to, but it was hard to see it in the moment. Had we stayed in Southern California, life would have been good. We dearly loved our friends and family there and, of course, still do. But sometimes you have to give up what you know for the new and next that God has planned. These past twenty-plus years in Atlanta have been truly life changing, and God's hand has been evident. Change can be difficult, but it's good, and, in fact, necessary. If you can't adapt to what is new, you can miss out on what God has planned.

Leadership is very similar. There are many reasons why as a leader you might resist change. You might be overwhelmed by what it would take to implement the change and can't imagine adding one more thing to your plate. Maybe the change threatens you or challenges your security. Or perhaps in a candid moment, you might say there's nothing wrong with the new and different, you just don't personally like it.

There are obviously some good reasons to resist change, such as you truly believe it would compromise your character or hurt the church. But the focus of this chapter is not how to stand up for what is right. The focus is on the necessity of change for every leader in order to grow, and how to adapt to that change in order to become more effective in your leadership.

When you learn to adapt rather than resist, your confidence rises. The move from San Diego to Atlanta taught me that you can make a change, but until you truly adapt and embrace it at a heart level, nothing is really different from the inside.

> When you learn to adapt rather than resist, your confidence rises.

There is something inside all of us that knows nothing stays the same forever. Yet we sometimes try to keep things as they are, even unknowingly. In general, we prefer the comfort and stability of what we already know. This gives us a greater sense of control. In contrast, change can make you feel like you are losing control, which attacks your confidence. And since the first gut-level response to change is a sense of what you're losing, to keep moving forward, it's crucial that you're able to switch the focus to what you are gaining.

Let's return to our narrative about David. It's amazing how much jumps out of his leadership story that communicates the importance of adaptability.

DAVID'S ABILITY TO ADAPT

Before David fled King Saul's palace, he'd only known two lives: as a poor shepherd, and then as Saul's son-in-law and commander in the his army. David's numerous military victories in that role made him stand out among the other generals and earned him the adoration of the people.

Yet, this very success in subduing Israel's enemies simultaneously fueled the king's insecurities. "Saul has slain his thousands, and David his tens of thousands," the women of Israel sang (1 Samuel 18:7).

Envious and paranoid, Saul's inflamed jealousy eventually exploded. David was suddenly on the run, in fear for his life, alone and stripped of all support and resources. A lesser man, in fact most men, would have been shattered by the devastating upheaval. But only rigid things shatter; flexible materials bend and shift under pressure without breaking. Over the next seven years, events would show David's character had strong levels of adaptability.

The first thing David did was what all wise men do when in a tough spot: he sought counsel. He fled to the prophet Samuel. But while Samuel took him in, it soon became apparent the prophet's protection would not last forever. David then changed strategies and sought help from Saul's own son Jonathan. But when an enraged Saul tried to kill even Jonathan, David ran again. This time, he ran to the priests serving at the tabernacle of God. But the priests were unable to offer David any more help than a weapon and some bread. He changed strategies again and ran to Saul's enemies for protection, the Philistines of Gath. But when the king of Gath was informed that David was the slayer of Goliath, David had to adapt to the situation and pretended to be crazy.

Over the next few years, David was somehow able to build a band of six hundred men and keep them fed and motivated, all while constantly evading capture by Saul's army in a territory the size of New Jersey.[1] Whether hiding in caves, living on the run, or leading a protection ring for local ranchers, David's conviction that he was not only willing but able to change and be whatever he needed to be to survive and move forward, greatly strengthened his confidence.

One thing he was *not* willing to adapt, however, were his principles. He never lifted a hand against King Saul in retribution. And for this, God would reward him with the kingship.

Leaders Go First

As a leader, you must be willing to change before you can lead others to do the same. The people you lead follow your example. They want to know that you have done or are willing to do what you ask them to do. That's a foundational element of character and it increases trust.

It's similar to what we all know is true in parenting. For example, when I asked my kids to put their smartphones away at dinner, they didn't want to see Dad sneaking a look at his phone either. I had to change first if I wanted to lead them to this new behavior. This example describes a specific behavior, but it also represents a value that family is important. When you want to lead a biblical value in your church and connect it to real behaviors, you, as the leader, must go first.

It's not always the case that what God asks of you he intends to ask of those you lead. In fact, more often than not, what God asks of you will be personal and just for you. He knows where you need to grow, change, and adapt. God wants to prepare you to lead at the next level.

Personal change is easier for some leaders than others. The more secure you are as a person and leader, the easier you're able to make

> **Personal change is easier for some leaders than others.**

the difficult changes that matter. Insecure leaders are tempted to change to please people, often in pursuit of comfort. In contrast, secure leaders intentionally change to influence people for the vision. Those who resist adapting to what is new, risk becoming stuck in both leadership and ministry. They therefore lose confidence, because not adapting won't work.

Seven-Step Process of Personal Change

1. Avoid Getting Stuck and Refuse to Stay Stuck

Small-group ministry has been around since the early church, but it continues to change in method. As a young pastor, I was trained in, and to this day believe in, an apprentice or multiplication model of small-group leadership. In that model, no group starts without an apprentice who commits to multiply to two groups within approximately eighteen months. That was our model at 12Stone Church for many years. However, we needed to make a change to accommodate rapid growth.

The decision was made to move to a semester-based model to provide more onboarding opportunities for people throughout the year. It was not an easy transition, but it was necessary because so many more people could get into a group faster and easier. If I had resisted it, I could have gotten stuck in my thinking and inadvertently caused the church to get stuck as well. The faster culture changes, the faster family lifestyles and time demands change, the more frequently we need to adapt how we offer ministry.

The best way to get stuck as a leader is to resist change, avoid adapting to new methods, and continue to lead in the same ways you have for the last several years. In short, when you stop growing you get stuck, which is a perfect recipe to kill your leadership confidence. The good news is if you do get stuck, you don't have to stay stuck. If you find that your ministry is stuck, the first place to look is at yourself, and ask the question, What needs to change?

2. Accept That Change Brings About Temporary Stress

Changing the ideology and methodology of small groups was personally stressful because I deeply believed in the model I knew. I was personally invested. It was even more stressful because we had trained several hundred volunteer leaders who believed in it as much as I did. Adapting to a semester model stretched us, but it was the best thing that could have happened for all of us who were leading, and more importantly, for the greater purpose of the church.

In time the stress was gone, and we celebrated thousands of new people growing in small groups. Since then we have continued to tweak and change our small-group methods and have learned how to better measure the big picture outcomes. Our focus is on life change, not any one particular method.

Church leadership is stressful on its own, so it's counterintuitive to embrace more stress, unless you know it's absolutely necessary to make progress in reaching more people for Christ. One important principle to remember is that the stress you experience going through healthy change is far less than the stress you will encounter if you don't change. And the better you learn to personally navigate these transitions, the greater your confidence becomes.

3. Ask God What He Has in Mind

What do you think needs to change at your church? What needs to change in the ministry you lead? How do you need to change and adapt personally to help make that happen?

Change is not a blind or random process. Smart change is guided by vision and purpose. I was talking with a young pastor named Drew who wanted some advice because his church was adopting a multisite model and he was asked to be a campus pastor. But he loved to preach and possessed an authentic confidence in his gift for communication, so he was considering becoming a senior pastor instead. He was grateful for the opportunity but knew it would greatly limit his ability to teach on Sundays.

He was torn because he loved his church and could easily see the great opportunity to reach more people, but he also wanted to teach. In this case, like my move from San Diego to Atlanta, Drew wasn't forced to adapt; he chose to. He chose to become a campus pastor because his vision to reach more people was greater than his vision to teach. When he prayed about it, that's exactly what God confirmed. Perhaps one day Drew will become a senior pastor, but for now, he asked God what he had in mind and the issue was settled. He told me that he'd have to adapt his thinking, but he was confident it was the right thing to do.

Asking God what he has in mind, along with keeping the vision before you, is essential to successfully adapting to personal change. And this always results in greater confidence.

4. Admit What's Holding You Back

Jeff was thirty years old, married, and had two young children. He was a global missions pastor and enjoyed his work, but he was also growing restless. Travel was becoming a hardship on his young family, but the real issue was that Jeff sensed a growing passion to become a professional licensed counselor. He hadn't told anyone for nearly three years.

As he told me his story, he admitted what had been holding him back. First, he was afraid he'd be perceived as a quitter. Jeff had made great declarations about the need for global evangelization. But while he still believed in that need, it was becoming less and less his personal calling. Second, his dad was a missionary and Jeff didn't want to disappoint him. Third, he had no idea how his family could afford for him to stop working and go back to school. These three things had been killing his confidence and caused him to hold back in silence. It was not until Jeff verbalized these things that he realized two reality-changing truths: none of them were good reasons not to become a counselor, and each of them had potential solutions.

One at a time he faced each fear. First, he spoke with his dad and told him his decision. It was a tough conversation, but his dad soon came around and was supportive. Then he confided in his personal friends as well as close colleagues on staff, including the senior pastor. Not one was judgmental or applied any guilt.

The third one was more complicated. There was no quick or obvious solution for how to go back to college and pay the tuition. Debt wasn't a good solution, and Jeff's wife going back to work with two young kids didn't make sense because childcare would consume much of what she could make.

The fear of what it would take to adapt to a new life in order to pursue a career in counseling shut them down for about a year. It wasn't until someone suggested they get more aggressive about scholarships and get serious about some unique work-from-home ideas for Jeff's wife that they gained enough confidence to go for it.

Getting honest about what is holding you back is a key step to moving forward, making changes, and adapting to your new next.

5. Adapt to What Is New

In late 2015, the 12Stone Church staff began the process of making a significant change in our ministry and corresponding staff structure. At that time, our main or broadcast campus carried the dual roles of campus leadership to grow the campus and of producing the ministry "product" for the other campuses. And by product, I mean the ministry design, materials, strategy, and content.

We embarked on the gigantic endeavor of adapting from a more decentralized model of multisite to a centralized model. We studied other churches long and hard, but when we started, it still felt like an expedition to the North Pole dressed in shorts and flip-flops. We had no idea what was in store.

We hired staff and our campus services department was born. I remember the first time we communicated the idea that a team from campus services would design and build the worship set for each of the campuses. More than one person looked at me like I was in serious need of a vacation.

Up-front collaboration was always the plan, but there were a number of questions and the team was cautiously optimistic. After some adjustments and trial and error, the campus teams and campus services were able to work together in an amazingly unified and productive way. But adapting to the new normal was difficult. Had we not kept the vision in front of us, we would not have successfully made it through the change. We learned that effective collaboration includes input on the front end and feedback on the back end.

> Effective collaboration includes input on the front end and feedback on the back end.

Words like *alignment* became the mantra. Teamwork was the consistent focus. But at the end of the day, what brought us through the tunnel were great relationships built on trust, mutual voluntary submission, and a focus on the mission.

I don't think a centralized model, where a central team designs, builds, and ships the product is ever easy. We work hard at it every day. But it's very rewarding when collaboration, trusting relationships, good teamwork, and alignment to the vision all come together.

When it's time for your team to adapt to an equally big change, give them time. Talk openly and honestly. And above all, make sure you're not the leader who is resisting needed change.

6. Allow Others to Speak into the Process

When John heard a call from God to step away from Skyline to teach leadership in churches across the country and globally, he asked me to go with him. For the next roughly seven years, we wrote materials, spoke to pastors and church leaders, and consulted for churches.

INJOY Ministries was growing rapidly, and John launched other ventures, including EQUIP, which continues today. I learned a lot, and sensed God using us to advance the kingdom while we helped church leaders become better at what they do.

I've always loved the church, and I'm a pastor at heart. In fall 2000, I began to sense a stir within me to return to a local church, and I was convinced I would be a senior pastor this time. I remember telling John, "I was your XP [executive pastor] and I loved it, but I don't think I'm doing that again. I believe I'm going to be a senior pastor." He just smiled and didn't say a word. I wasn't ready to listen or hear anything different. And neither John nor I was interested in a change in our ministry partnership and personal relationship. We talked about it for nearly a year, all the while loving what we were doing to help pastors and churches.

Patti was the first to say, "Hun, you'd be a great senior pastor, but I think you were designed to be an XP." Then, a month or so later, John said the same thing. A couple of others close to me chimed in with the same message. Then God made it clear in a 2:00 a.m. prayer. He told me I would be an XP again, and, in fact, he had a clear plan. Listening to trusted advisors had increased my confidence, especially when confirmed by God.

It was becoming quite clear that I needed to listen and allow others to speak into this process. By fall 2001, I was the XP of 12Stone Church, and it clearly has been God's plan. I can't imagine what may have happened if I had refused to listen to others. I had to adapt to a new way of thinking and a new plan. And I'm glad I did.

7. Assess for Clear Progress

You are never at the mercy of change. You may not feel like it was your idea, or that you orchestrated the change, or even wanted it, but now that it's here, you need to take charge of the change. The same thing is true if it was your idea. In either case, take responsibility for all that is new.

This includes a variety of things, from a positive attitude to a clear new vision. But one of the best things to do is assess your progress. To do this, you need to establish clear goals. What does the new and improved look like? What are your opportunities for personal growth and improvement for the church? Never waste the stress of change. As a leader, you don't want to work for change, you want change to work for you. That means you don't burn all your energy into the change itself. Instead, leverage your effort for a better future.

> You are never at the mercy of change.

Don't waste time looking back. Keep pressing forward. This includes connecting and integrating chapters 8 and 9 together. They are intentionally designed to be embraced as a pair in your process of growth. Adaptability can be seen as movement from left to right, and improvement can be seen as movement both up and down.

As we continue to move through the process of developing authentic confidence, change and adaptability, when genuinely embraced, open a new vista for improvement.

CHAPTER 9

IMPROVEMENT

AIM FOR BETTER, NOT BIGGER

It's not all about talent. It's about dependability,
consistency, and being able to improve. If you
work hard and are coachable, and you understand
what you need to do, you can improve.

—BILL BELICHICK

The road from obscurity to a global NBA superstar was not easy, but it was the journey Steph Curry embraced.

Stephen "Steph" Curry was born on March 14, 1988, in Akron, Ohio, and fell in love with basketball at an early age.[1] Little did he imagine he would become one of the greatest shooters of all time, a skill that would be developed through a combination of hard work, discipline, and a dedication to improvement.

The Currys were a close family, and Steph and his brother, Seth, attended a Montessori school founded by his mother.[2] His parents were both athletes. His dad, Dell, was an NBA shooting guard and his mom, Sonya, was a Virginia Tech volleyball player. However, his talent was not merely a product of genetics.

Steph's drive began when he was young. He built upon what was passed on to him from his parents and took it to the next level through a willingness to work at it diligently.[3]

As a child, Steph learned to shoot on a makeshift basketball hoop his grandfather built. The rustic nature of the basket forced Steph to get the ball straight through the hoop, while his ball-handling skills were developed and improved because of his grandparents' muddy and rock-filled yard. Years later a concrete half court with an NBA-grade basket would be built at his home in Ohio, but Steph would always prefer the challenges of a rough yard and a basket with a flimsy backboard.[4]

If you'd known Steph in high school, you would have likely seen a skinny teenager with the skills and drive of a professional. NBA players often practice by shooting hundreds of jump shots each day, but even in these younger years, Curry would typically take up to a thousand jump shots during a single practice.[5] As a result, he became a fantastic shooter.

Unfortunately, despite achieving a phenomenal shooting percentage from behind the three-point arc, he was not offered a single college scholarship from a major conference school. Under the weight of that disappointment, many players would have tossed in the towel, but for Steph, it only motivated him even more.

Throughout Steph's college career, he continued to improve his shooting skills and stats, and even garnered several individual awards. He finally caught the attention of the NBA as a college sophomore. But for the scouts, he was still a long shot.[6] Most thought Steph was too small, not athletic enough, or that he had fragile "glass" ankles. He conquered all those criticisms by living out his four core ideals: faith, passion, drive, and will.[7] He was the seventh pick of the Golden State Warriors in the first round in 2009.[8]

In 2015, the NBA awarded Steph Curry its annual MVP award. In his acceptance speech, he spoke about these ideals. Greater than his confidence in himself, though, as a devout Christian, he had great faith in God, and his passion for the game gave him the drive to improve every single day.

After reading about Steph Curry, it's my hunch that he drove himself to be better every day. The strength of his will helped him to press through setbacks and challenges.

In 2016, Steph won the NBA's MVP Award for a second consecutive year in a row, and he is the only player in the league's history to have won by unanimous vote.[9] A stellar accomplishment resulting from his commitment to improve. Steph's goal was never to become a bigger name but to become a better player.

Improvement Is an Element of Stewardship

God gave you gifts, talents, and abilities. He's also given you dreams, desires, and opportunities. What you do with all that is up to you. As a good steward of what you've been given, you likely want to make the most of it. We all have "glass ankles" of some kind. Even Superman contended with kryptonite. But equally true is your potential to improve, no matter what your limitations may be. When you fully embrace the larger vision of God's work and your calling to lead, improvement becomes a matter of stewardship.

When you care about those you lead, you naturally want to improve as a leader to serve them better. One of my favorite things to ask of a leader is to complete this sentence: "I would be a better leader if I _____
_____."

It's a very revealing question. It also quickly communicates the leader's focus on improvement. If he or she can immediately give me a confident answer, there is a much higher likelihood that the leader is working on getting better. Further, depending on the specific answer, it sheds light on the leader's level of self-awareness. How about you? How would you fill in that blank?

Resist the Temptation for Bigger over Better

As church leaders, we live in a seven-day cycle of either joy or disappointment. Every Sunday we face the attendance of our churches. We know life change is what really matters, and that's obviously true. But I've never met an honest leader who says they love it when their attendance is low. And I've never met a pastor who prayed and asked God for just a few less people to show up next Sunday. It's easy to allow your strategy to become more about building a bigger crowd than developing better leaders, including yourself.

In the short run, you can boost your attendance. But it will always come back down unless you focus on becoming a better and more confident leader and trust that your church will grow as you do, in combination with God's favor.

The same principle is true for you personally. Resist the temptation to build a big network, gain more followers on social media, or create an impressive platform for yourself. Don't get me wrong, bigger isn't bad. But get better before you get bigger. If you put bigger first, you may never get better. If you put better first, God will likely help you get bigger.

Choose Community over Isolation

Improvement never flourishes in isolation. Whether you're a church staff member, a pro athlete, or a businessperson, operating in relative isolation is never a good idea. "Relative isolation" means that being surrounded by people doesn't ensure you're in community.

The temptation for leaders to work detached from others is real, sometimes seemingly out of necessity. In a small church, for example, it may appear that you're alone in your leadership. For others in larger churches, it's amazingly easy to hide in a crowd of people. Either way, the perception that there is no one to let in or to choose not to let others in, has an equally negative impact on your ability to improve. Further, authentic confidence only comes from the vulnerability that exists in authentic community.

Develop your team of insiders, truth tellers, and trusted advisors. If you lead a small church that's not physically near other larger churches, it's worth driving the distance on a regular basis. Find a couple of pastors or Christian business leaders who have greater experience and have led a slightly larger community than you currently do. Ask them to meet every other month for an hour; quarterly works well too. If you lead in a large setting, the same principle is true. Just two or three of these coaches and mentors can help you realize significant improvement. Respect their time, be prepared with good questions, and put their advice to practice. Each time you meet, always begin by letting them know what you implemented from the previous conversation and how it went.

In addition, family and friends are at the core of your community. Open up to those who care about you and have the strength to tell you the truth. They know you the best and therefore have the potential to help you the most.

> **Authentic community doesn't require dozens of people.**

Authentic community doesn't require dozens of people. If you have just five smart, strong people—between family, friends, and advisors—who make up your trusted insiders, you are blessed and set up well to improve. And there's nothing quite like obvious improvement to strengthen your leadership confidence.

In our Old Testament story about David, it's fascinating to see that even while on the run and with emotions trending high, he still found a way to improve.

DAVID IMPROVES ON THE RUN

While on the run, David watched God miraculously save him again and again. After Saul died in battle against the Philistines, the people of Israel turned to David as Saul's natural replacement, exactly as God had foreordained would happen.

Once established on the throne, David's heart led him to honor *his* King, the God of Israel. He instinctively wanted God close to him.

The tabernacle was considered to be God's house and the site of his physical presence on earth. Associated with it were many sacred objects, but none of them approached the ark of the covenant, the *most* sacred religious object in all Israel—and really all of human history. It was considered the footstool of God's throne (1 Chronicles 28:2) and earthly reflection of another ark in God's heavenly temple (Revelation 11:19).

David sought to honor God by bringing both the tabernacle and the ark to Jerusalem. He gave orders to begin the process: "They set the ark of God on a new cart . . . [and] Uzzah and Ahio, sons of Abinadab, were guiding the new cart with the ark of God on it" (2 Samuel 6:3–4).

Then, everything fell apart. It's often said the road to hell is paved with good intentions. "Uzzah reached out and took hold of the ark of God, because the oxen stumbled. The Lord's anger burned against Uzzah because of his irreverent act; therefore God struck him down, and he died there beside the ark of God" (2 Samuel 6:6–7).

David was angry and afraid. Failure shakes every leader's confidence. He froze the procession and stored the ark, asking, "How can the ark of the Lord ever come to me?" (2 Samuel 6:9). Thankfully, David's character was that he was not only able to sustain adaptability, but he was also able to work to improve himself. He sought outside counsel and discovered that while his heart had been right, he'd failed to align his procedure with what God had previously said: "When the camp is to move, Aaron and his sons . . . must not touch the holy things, or they will die. [They] are to carry those things [on poles] that are in the tent of meeting" (Numbers 4:5–6, 15).

In faith, David tried again. Gone were the cart and oxen that could stumble and spill the holy chest onto the dirt; now holy men carried it on poles. This time they made it to Jerusalem with David rejoicing and worshipping before the ark the entire way.

David was willing to adapt and improve, which are like the right and left gloves for change resulting in growth. This is a powerful lesson for all of us and vital for the development of our character and confidence. Let me tell you the story of another David and his road to improvement.

A Conversation with David Drury

David Drury was raised in Marion, Indiana, a union town of forty thousand people flanked by cornfields and automakers. He was raised in an evangelistic church that placed strong emphasis on reaching out. As an elementary student, he heard an announcement for backyard Bible clubs and thought he would lead one in his rustic tree house.

David had no idea that the leadership invitation was intended only for adults. He felt confident he was a leader, so he thought why not? The cool thing is that the church let him, and by the end of the week, he led one of the kids to Christ.

David later interned at a church in Michigan where he met, dated, and married his wife, Kathy, before moving to Boston. After completing his graduate work at Gordon Conwell, the couple planted a successful church back in Indianapolis. David was just twenty-three years old. Wanting to plant another one, he raised up a new leader, handed the church off to him, and was off to Bloomington-Normal, Illinois, at the age of twenty-five. This experience, however, did not go as well. After eighteen months of struggles with church planting, David felt like a failure and his confidence was crushed.

In retrospect, David confided that he needed to learn what to do with failure.[10] God used that experience to teach him those valuable lessons. Thankfully, the next two churches went better.

First, David joined a staff in a healthy and growing church and led small-group leaders for the next five years. Following that, he became the executive pastor at College Church in Marion, Indiana. It was here that he began to embrace a calling to second chair leadership. Today, David serves as chief of staff for the Wesleyan Church, where he has been for the last seven years.

That time of brokenness following his second church plant forced David to figure out how to improve. And being a natural leader, he intuitively knew he wasn't going to get better alone. David is a really smart guy. He figured out that being a natural leader had its advantages, but it also had a downside. The disadvantage was, because he could naturally do ministry well, he didn't know how to get better. David told me, "I'm pretty sure I didn't improve from seventeen to twenty-seven years of age. I just kept leading the same way."[11]

> "If you want to go fast, go alone. If you want to go far, go together."
> —DAVID DRURY

An old saying stuck with David: "If you want to go fast, go alone. If you want to go far, go together." To improve as a leader, he wisely began to find mentors to pick their brains and learn from them. He wanted to get better; he *had* to get better.

One of the first skills he improved was learning how to scale as a leader. His job as a small groups pastor in a church of fifteen hundred required him to recruit and train exponentially more leaders than his previous church plant of forty people. David found leaders who were already present and learned like crazy. This grew his confidence as well.

Another area in which David wanted to improve was his communication. He was confident speaking to a crowd of up to two hundred but lacked confidence speaking to larger crowds of more than one thousand. He found mentors who were better communicators than he was and sat with them as they reviewed videos of his teaching, picking it apart line by line. He learned quickly that it's always fun when your mentor pushes pause at the second line of your talk and says, "I think I know what you were *trying* to do there." It requires the same kind of vulnerability and nakedness as standing in a doctor's office with nothing on but that thin gown open in the back. Despite being woefully uncomfortable, those experiences helped David get better and walk onto a large stage with confidence.

This surprised me because I see David as a naturally confident leader. So I asked him where his confidence came from. He said, "The sovereignty of God. I've always just believed God has me and it will all work out." But digging a little further, he added, "When I learned to prepare and began to do work in advance of a meeting or a speaking event, my confidence became more authentic and consistent. It was so much better than bluffing my way through just because I could."[12]

Like David, we all need to improve. As life is not a constant, what's required of you and your confidence is not constant either. Improvement is a lifelong endeavor, and the following plan will help you make the most of the time you invest in your personal growth.

Four Steps to Improvement and Increased Confidence

1. Think

I love asking leaders when they think. The quick answer is usually something like, "All the time." But that's not true. They don't think all the time. I don't and you don't either. No one does. In fact, it's amazing how much we, as leaders, can do on autopilot. We just repeat what we've done over and over again, which never results in improvement. Nor does it help the church make progress.

Set aside time to think. Specifically, this includes things like testing new thoughts, solving new problems, connecting different ideas for innovative improvement, and assessing what to do with all that to make it useful. This requires honest self-assessment about where you need to improve. You may consider a long list of things you want or need to improve in, but it's vital that you shorten the list to a manageable maximum of three things. One at a time is preferable.

> **Set aside time to think.**

Then, add time in your calendar. There is no right or wrong plan. An hour a day might work for you. Maybe you would do better with twenty minutes each morning and one four-hour block a week. Experiment and do what works for you. If you're not sure where to begin in terms of what to focus on, start with problems you're trying to solve and how you need to improve to lead your ministry forward.

2. Learn

Thinking and learning should go hand in hand. You may prefer listening to podcasts, engaging in a classroom environment, participating in a roundtable discussion, or reading blog posts. I appreciate all of these, but I especially love reading books. I still like to hold a physical book in my hands and mark it up as I dive in and mine for the gold. Some books are loaded with wisdom and others have just one nugget. But that one nugget might be life changing. The authors' thoughts stimulate new thoughts that expand my learning.

> **For leaders, learning is a lifestyle.**

For leaders, learning is a lifestyle. It's part of what is required and has a tremendous effect on your level of confidence. But for that to happen, and for the new information to become transformational, you need to take action. That doesn't mean you act on everything you learn. Again, prioritize what you're learning so that you can improve the specific areas that will give you the most needed and productive results. This requires practice.

3. Practice

Stephen Curry didn't become an NBA superstar without lots and lots of practice. And even though he's considered to be among the best of the best shooters, he still keeps practicing. He practices against a scoreboard, a time clock, and an opposing team. That's how he gets better.

Likewise, you can't merely practice in your mind. Practicing in the reality of daily leadership and against real organizational goals is how you make the greatest improvement.

Perhaps you need to practice your communication and recruiting skills as David Drury did, or maybe you need to practice your style of inspiring others to action or developing and empowering leaders to lead. There's really no end to the possibilities.

It's also important to make practice an enjoyable process. It's best to see practice as a great opportunity to improve, not merely as more work to do. There was a time when I was practicing guitar on a regular basis. I secretly wanted to be the lead guitar player for a U2 tour, so I had to be able to outplay the Edge! In addition to being delusional, I made practice all work. It was no longer fun and so I quit practicing, and Bono never did call.

> It's always more fun to lead when you're a better leader.

That didn't mean I wouldn't go after something difficult to play, because I did. But I lost sight of the bigger picture, which was simply enjoying being a better guitar player.

This is easy to do in leadership too. Don't lose sight of the fact that it's always more fun to lead when you're a better leader. The practice is worth it.

4. Feedback

Very few leaders can improve without some coaching, because we don't know how to improve without feedback. I'm not much of a cook, but on occasion I try to improve my very rudimentary culinary skills. What seems simple isn't, when you don't know how. Patti is a fantastic cook, and she coaches me from time to time. Actually, her first instinct is to coach me out of the kitchen, but then I tell her I really want to learn and improve, so she usually agrees to let me stay.

For example, I often make eggs for breakfast, but I couldn't figure out why they were either burning because they were sticking to the pan or took so long to cook they were like rubber. I tried several heat settings, but nothing seemed to work. When I finally consulted with Patti she said, "Cook eggs low and slow and use more butter." That was it. My eggs are awesome now, and I'm much more confident about making them.

That's what a good leadership coach or mentor can do for you. This person may be your boss, a businessperson, a pastor of another church, a friend who mentors you, or a professional paid coach. All these options work great. You don't need to meet often, but you do need to be intentional about it. As I mentioned earlier in this chapter, come prepared with questions, practice what you talked about, and the next time you meet, talk about what you did, what worked, and what didn't work.

As you adapt and improve, you will surely face new pressures and experience setbacks. That's the nature of growth and change. Your confidence may take a hit during the change, but you can bounce back. The next chapter takes you through that process of developing resilience.

CHAPTER 10

RESILIENCE

HANDLE PRESSURE WELL AND BOUNCE BACK

You may have to fight a battle more than once to win it.
—Margaret Thatcher

Pressures, problems, and pushbacks are all part of any leader's life. And leading within the context of the church is no exception. When you add theology, personal faith, and people's passion for certain ministries to the mix, the conflicts can at times get intense. The need for resilience to reside deep in your character is necessary to sustain successful leadership and the confidence you desire over the long haul.

Attempting to construct a new building or expand a current one is a common story of resistance, opposition, and setbacks in the church. Perhaps you have a story of your own. The list of typical hurdles to overcome in this scenario is long. For example, nearby neighbors don't want a church or the traffic it will bring to their town. Zoning issues get complicated quickly. City officials can make the permit process difficult. Then, there are surprises like discovering a rock that has to be blown up or environmentally sensitive habitats that may be disturbed and therefore require expensive solutions. Then there's the always challenging question of how to pay for the building in the first place. Many people leave churches during building campaigns and return when they're done.

Not to mention that all those things just represent the pressure a building endeavor can bring into play while everything else must continue as usual. This includes things like preparing a sermon each week, making sure volunteers are serving happily in their respective ministries, keeping all the technology working all the time, staying on budget with every project, and, of course, serving a coffee that pleases everyone. You can't weather this kind of leadership journey without resilience being part of your makeup as a leader.

Let me tell you a story of a friend of mine named Carey who went through a leadership crucible and came out the other side with a spirit of resiliency.

A Conversation with Carey Nieuwhof

Carey's book *Didn't See It Coming* is a great description of the burnout that caught him by surprise eleven years into his ministry.

Born to parents who were Dutch immigrants, Carey grew up in Windsor, Ontario. His dad worked hard in the tool- and mold-making industry, eventually owning his own business. Watching the hustle and dedication of both his father and grandfather, who worked as a janitor and truck driver, taught Carey much about a strong work ethic at a young age. Of them, he said, "Watching my parents make their way in this country taught me a lot about resilience."[1]

This work ethic paid off for Carey later, earning him three degrees by the time he was thirty: a bachelor's degree, a law degree, and a seminary degree. Even after processing a call to ministry, Carey worked for a year in a law firm, confiding, "I wasn't sure ministry was for me."[2]

Yet, in the middle of seminary in 1995, Carey accepted a call to become a student pastor. God placed him in a three-point charge, meaning he was asked to serve three different historic Presbyterian churches at the same time, each congregation then averaging fewer than thirty people in attendance. Some of these people would go on to launch Connexus Church, a Northpoint Strategic Partner, which is thriving today, and where Carey is the founding pastor. But the road to get there was difficult.

The three tiny churches began to grow, and they were running out of space, so Carey began to change things. Feathers were ruffled, to say the least. These churches were filled with wonderful people, but they also had the typical problems, from a choir that couldn't really sing to lay leaders who commonly said, "This is how we do it here." For generations, their children had been born there, baptized, married, and so forth. There was too much history for them to embrace change lightly.

Not shockingly, when Carey began the process of selling the three buildings to merge into one larger space, he encountered tremendous resistance. The people got truly angry. One gentleman told Carey, "I'm so mad at you I'm not going to allow you to do my funeral!" Now *that* is angry.

Through all this, Carey held steady, but it began to wear him down. He told me, "I started a slide toward burnout. My resilience was strong for the first eleven years, but people told me that I would burn out at my current pace and load. I told them 'I won't burn out.' And I was wrong."[3]

In May 2006, his body finally gave out. He lost his passion, drive, and motivation. He still got out of bed every day and headed to work, but he had no energy and could no longer feel his faith. His confidence was all but gone.

That July, Carey took three weeks off to rest and regroup, but he returned even worse. It was then that he knew the situation was serious. The elders wanted him to take a sabbatical, but he wouldn't because he sensed if he left, he'd never come back. Nevertheless, the church helped him through it. With a reduced workload and a lot of counseling and prayer, he finally felt a flicker of hope in his spirit after about five months.

For a time, Carey focused his energy on grieving his losses, working on performance issues, and recuperating from physical exhaustion caused by doing too much for more than a decade. It was a slow recovery, but in a year, he was 80 percent back to normal.

Still, "normal" had gotten him burned out. Knowing this to be true, Carey set out to learn a new normal, a healthy one with boundaries, limits, and smart rhythms. He had a new way to handle his time, energy, and priorities. In fact, that was more than fourteen years ago, and Carey reports having more energy now in his fifties than he did in his younger years.

Carey has always been a great leader, but now he is also a leader who can go the distance with endurance. His hard work and resilience have paid off.

When I asked Carey about his confidence as a leader, he shared, "I'm still finding it. It's a dance. Prior to burnout, I would have said my confidence was strong, at least on the outside. On the inside, however, I was searching because of my insecurities. As I mentioned, I was never sure I belonged or fit in ministry. I was probably afraid of not performing successfully, and I felt insecure around people more successful than me. As my personal security has increased, it's been easier to let go and my confidence has risen."[4]

Today, Carey hosts a podcast where he continually lifts others up. He likes to feature their gifts, strengths, and contributions to others. Since 1995, those three little churches have merged, transformed, built buildings, and left buildings. Now Connexus is an amazing church that continues to reach out to the lost and have tremendous impact on the kingdom.

Handling Pressure and Problems and Living to Tell About It

If you are leading, there is no way to escape pressure. If you are successful, you feel pressure. If you fail, you feel pressure. And if you coast, you still deal with pressure.

Problems are just part of the leadership landscape, and not all problems are negative. They are often part of progress. Think of it this way: Leaders cause motion, motion causes friction, and people resist friction. Change is always at the core of the issue.

> If you are leading, there is no way to escape pressure.

Here's another quick perspective. Change is necessary, leaders create change to make progress, but people don't like change. Nevertheless, even though problems and the pressure they bring are just part of the process, knowing that doesn't reduce the toll they will take on you as a leader. Your ability to handle pressure is vitally important to sustained, authentic confidence.

Two Sources of Pressure

Your ability to identify the source of your pressure sets you up to handle it better. There are two primary sources.

1. Internal Pressure

Internal pressure is the pressure you put on yourself. There are both positive and negative elements connected to this kind of pressure. The positive element is a result of personal characteristics such as high standards, personal discipline, and the desire to succeed. These are all good if not taken to extremes. After all, personal drive is necessary to lead, and self-motivation is required to make progress in the mission of the church.

However, the negative element comes from things like fear and insecurity (covered in chapter 2), which often result in the pointless pursuit of pleasing people or getting caught in the performance trap. In short, fear causes you to believe you may fail, and insecurity makes you believe you aren't good enough and can't do it.

As you read and reflect on your internal pressure, would you describe it as largely positive or negative in nature? If it leans toward the negative, how might you change that?

2. External Pressure

External pressure is the pressure others and the organization itself place on you. Like internal pressure, there are both positive and negative aspects. The positive aspect reflects the reality that there is simply a great deal of work to be done to see the church move forward. Taking ownership to see the church grow is a healthy external pressure.

A negative version of external pressure is taking on too much, overworking to get it all done, ending up over your head, and living in frustration. Yes, there are internal elements connected to this, but the pressure I'm referring to originates from things like financial shortfalls and conflict with those who disagree with the direction or even someone you report to.

We'll return to the practical aspects of handling pressure, but first, let's

> A negative version of external pressure is taking on too much.

turn to one last narrative of David, where both internal and external pressures are seen, as well as his resilience to keep going.

DAVID'S RESILIENCE

"As King David approached Bahurim, a man from the same clan as Saul's family came out from there. His name was Shimei son of Gera, and . . . he pelted David and all the king's officials with stones . . . Shimei said, "Get out, get out, you murderer, you scoundrel!" (2 Samuel 16:5–7).

Each stone struck David so much deeper than just pain in his flesh. Though done in the name of perceived injustice against Saul, when David heard "you murderer," he almost certainly thought of Uriah, Bathsheba's husband.

After falling into adultery with her and covering it up with Uriah's murder, the prophet Nathan formally pronounced God's judgment. David would harvest four times the sin he would sow (2 Samuel 12:1–6).

Specifically, his punishment was to suffer the loss of four sons. First, the baby he'd conceived with Bathsheba died. Then, his beloved son Absalom murdered his half-brother, Amnon, after Amnon raped Absalom's sister Tamar. For this, Absalom was forced into exile.

Out of love for his son, though, David eventually welcomed him back home. But Absalom didn't return the kindness. While smiling before the king's face, he built a conspiracy behind his back, secretly stealing the hearts of the men of Israel. When the plot was ripe, Absalom seized the throne, and David and his men fled for their lives.

As they crossed the Mount of Olives and descended toward the Jordan River, David and his people wept. David walked barefoot and covered his head in mourning while Shimei cast contemptuous rocks at him and his friends (2 Samuel 15:30). He knew either his son or his kingdom would soon be dead. Both could no longer simultaneously exist.

David's men wanted to stop Shimei's cursing, but David said, "Leave him alone; let him curse, for the LORD has told him to. It may be that the LORD will look upon my misery and restore to me his covenant blessing instead of his curse today" (2 Samuel 16:11–12).

Here we catch a glimpse of the resilience God had embedded deep in David's character—deeper than any rock could reach. Rather than rejoice when Absalom was killed, David mourned all the more. But when he realized his people needed to see him strong, he shook himself out of his grief and "got up and took his seat in the gateway" (2 Samuel 19:8). Resilience was deep within him, and it gave him the confidence he needed to reign, even in the face of the most devastating tragedies.

As a leader, you will face hardships and pressure like David, and resilience is needed to press on. Learning how to handle that pressure is vital to your confidence as a leader.

The Anatomy of Pressure

When you begin in ministry, you start off with low pressure and high margin. But in time, you will inevitably have high pressure and low margin. Every time you add something to your life, such as a mortgage, a child, or another campus, you add pressure and reduce margin. This is not bad in itself; it's simply part of life. A deeper understanding of this

> When you begin in ministry, you start off with low pressure and high margin. But in time, you will inevitably have high pressure and low margin.

process will help you become more resilient, which increases your confidence.

- *Pressure is always about more.* Leaders always create more. Church growth is inherently about more—more people, more challenges, and thankfully, more stories of life change.

- *More affects your margin.* Unless you have an unknown superpower and wear a cool costume, you have natural limits. The lower your margin, the closer you get to your limit. Richard Swenson defined margin as "the space between our load and our limits."[5]
- *The reduction of your margin increases your pressure.* Margin is your time to think, rest, play, dream, plan, and create. When you squeeze your margin so you don't have time for these essentials, or perhaps even for your family, your pressure shoots through the roof and your confidence drops through the floor.
- *Pressure left unregulated drains your resilience and reduces your capacity.* You can endure lots of pressure for a short period of time. But sustained pressure will undo even the strongest of leaders because we all have a breaking point.

> Margin is your time to think, rest, play, dream, plan, and create.

The goal isn't to avoid pressure and gain massive margin. That's not possible in a growing church or organization of any size. If you want low pressure and lots of margin, you need to be in a small, no-growth environment. But that, too, in time, will bring pressures of its own due to lack of growth. The goal is to improve and increase your ability to handle pressure and to regulate it, especially in low-margin seasons.

Five Ways to Handle Pressure in a Healthy Way

1. Get Your Perspective Right

Like a good doctor, you need to get the diagnosis right to be effective. But it's difficult to see things accurately when you're under pressure with so much to do. For example, I've had many staff members come to me over the years and say they're working something like sixty-five to seventy hours a week. I always respond by saying, "That's way too much. Let's take a closer look at what you're doing." We then dig into their calendar to get an accurate look. Sometimes the staff person *is* working too much, or possibly way too much, and we focus on solving that problem.

More often than not, however, they're not overworking at the church. The reality is, they have a very busy life. They just have a ton going on all the time between the kids, the car in the shop, the extra bills to pay, someone being sick, work, family celebrations, household chores and repairs, and the list goes on. Here's why this distinction is important. If you are working too much at the church, that's a problem that involves a specific solution church leadership should help provide. However, if you are not overworking, but instead you have a super-busy life, a very different solution is required. That difference in perspective is a game changer!

How you think about and approach your situation makes all the difference. For example, it may not be an external pressure as I just described. For you it might be more internal pressure in the form of expectations created by fear or insecurity. Start with an accurate diagnosis and a right perspective.

2. Tend to Your Soul

Let God carry what you can't carry. If you are like me, you may tend to think you can handle more than you were designed to carry. About fifteen years ago we were involved in some very complicated financial and land use issues in preparation to build a large auditorium seating twenty-five hundred people.

That summer, anxiety came out of nowhere. I became overwhelmed just sitting at my desk, and spontaneous heart palpitations made my heart race. This continued for a couple of weeks, and my confidence was depleting. I broke in a church board meeting and had no idea what was going on. They said it was too much pressure unanswered for too long and prayed for me. Their kindness was healing even in the moment. I smile now as I remember saying, "What pressure?" I was so clueless that I foolishly had not protected any margin. Further, I overextended my capacity to carry a heavy load and refused to face the reality of human limits. Fortunately, I called a brilliant counselor I had known for years in San Diego, and in about three months, the anxiety was gone and has not returned. I had to be reminded that I needed to let God carry what I could not carry.

My daily rhythm included exercise and prayer, but play and margin

> Let God carry what you can't carry.

were absent. I continue to work at including both. I may not ever excel at margin and play, but the progress has made a huge difference. How about you? Are you tending to your soul?

3. Know Your Healthy Pressure-Relief Valve

Pressure often causes a leader to seek relief in unhealthy ways. The list of possibilities is long and includes things like overeating, overspending, and binge-watching TV. From there it can morph to self-medicating, and get worse as it goes.

I was addicted to sugar and didn't know it. For decades I consumed more chocolate chip cookies and Godiva chocolate than you could ever imagine. It wasn't until a doctor told me that my A1C was approaching pre-diabetic levels that I got a wake-up call and cut 80 to 90 percent of my sugar intake overnight. That was about five years ago, and I hope to never go back.

We all need what I call pressure-relief valves, but they must be healthy ones. I mentioned that play is not my spiritual gift. Don't misunderstand, I love to play. I'm just not likely to initiate it. I have to be intentional about it and so do you. How do you play? What's fun for you? I don't mean everyday playfulness. That's great and hopefully it's part of your life. I mean, how do you play in a way that restores your soul?

Personality plays a part in this process. For example, whether you are an introvert or extrovert will determine what helps you relax and have fun. My wife is an introvert and needs alone time to restore her soul. She's strong and fun and most people think she's an extrovert, but I can see the signs when her battery is draining. She just needs a few quiet hours with a great book or some time at the beach to recharge.

Vacation is universally good for everyone, but that can't be the only answer. What restores you that is easily accessible, doesn't cost too much, and fits into your daily or weekly rhythms?

4. Right-Size the Problem

If you think the mountain is too big to climb, it is. If that image is multiplied by numerous problems or multiple big mountains to climb, the effect is like a prize fighter pounding on your confidence.

When you face problems and setbacks and the pressure that comes with them, it's easy to "oversize" the problem. This is just as big an issue as underestimating the problem, and more common when you're under pressure.

A children's staff member said to me, "I have to recruit a ton of volunteers this summer." She was stressed to the max and felt huge pressure. I asked, "How many do you need?" She looked surprised and said she didn't know. I asked her to figure that out and let me know the number in two days. She did, and the number was something like thirty-nine volunteers for the summer. She smiled and said, "I can do that for sure." When she right-sized the problem, her pressure dropped and confidence rose.

A senior pastor called stressed about the fact that he needed to raise $2.5 million for a capital campaign. He'd never been responsible for raising that much money before and felt overwhelmed. I asked how much he raised at the same church during the last campaign, and he told me it was $1.5 million. I said to him, "So with God's help, you're confident about your ability to raise $1.5 million. Right?" He agreed. I continued by saying, "This time you need to raise $2.5 million. Let's right-size this. Your leadership growth gap is about raising an additional $1 million, but the congregation is larger, the giving is up, and the momentum is strong." He quickly grasped the concept of right-sizing the problem and felt more at ease.

> A key part of the formula is to determine what you can do and not get stuck focusing on what you can't do.

A key part of the formula is to determine what you can do and not get stuck focusing on what you can't do. Sometimes the pressure is still intense even after right-sizing the problem. When you are clear about the things you can't control or can't do, let them go. You are wasting energy carrying that burden. Instead, focus on what you can do.

5. Lean In to It

There are times—God-ordained times—when the pressure is high and your margin is low, and God wants you to lean in to it. He uses those moments to stretch you and grow your resilience and capacity. This is a healthy process if you have the previous four points operating at least moderately well in your life. In fact, it's often a composite of getting your perspective right, tending to your soul, knowing and practicing your healthy relief valve, and right-sizing your problems. Then you are ready to lean in to leading at a new level with the confidence to match.

A longtime friend and colleague, Chris Huff, shared with me that when he ran his first marathon, his running mentor told him, "When you are spent and completely done, and your mind thinks your body can't do it anymore, it can." On occasion, in certain seasons, God will ask you to run a leadership marathon. If you are in good shape mentally, physically, spiritually, and emotionally, you can do more than you think. However, setting yourself up to be healthy is yours to own. The principles and practices in this chapter will help you develop the resilience you need to finish the race.

You will always face new pressures and experience setbacks, but resilience and the confidence that comes with it will help you make it through.

These first ten chapters have focused on the internal aspects of your leadership confidence with an emphasis on application. The remaining five chapters will focus on daily practical disciplines. These are five of the primary big-picture functions of leadership and how they connect to the development of your confidence.

PART 3

DAILY PRACTICAL DISCIPLINES

A dream does not become a reality through magic;
it takes sweat, determination, and hard work.
—COLIN POWELL

D r. John Maxwell was speaking to a crowd of about two thousand leaders. Toward the end of the day, while he was signing books, a gentleman walked up to him and said, "I'd like to do what you do." John's response was, "Would you like to do what I did, so you can do what I do?"[1]

That's the question of a lifetime. John basically challenged him with the question of whether he was willing to pay the price to realize his dream. John certainly had to put in the hard work to realize his dreams. He grew up in a middle-American community of Circleville, Ohio. His parents were wonderful influencers in his early life. John's earliest childhood memory was that he thought he would someday be a preacher.

In 1969, John completed his bachelor's degree, married Margaret, and moved to tiny, rural Hillham, Indiana, where he began his first position as a senior pastor. He would go on to lead two more churches, Faith Memorial in Lancaster, Ohio, and Skyline Wesleyan in San Diego, California, for a total of twenty-five years.

From there, he would follow God's call to develop more leaders by launching many impressive endeavors, including EQUIP, the John Maxwell Company, the John Maxwell Team, and the John Maxwell Leadership Foundation.

Most people know John as a gifted visionary leader, motivational speaker, and bestselling author with more than ninety books to his name. He is that and more.

John travels the world and consults with presidents, CEOs, and other high-capacity leaders. He pours out his energy to influence entire countries. He is a devoted father, wonderful grandfather, loving husband, and incredible friend. I'm blessed to be among those he has personally mentored, and we have shared a deep friendship for nearly forty years.

What I can tell you about John that you may not know is what motivates him and keeps him going. In a recent conversation, he shared with me the story of when he was in his twenties and decided he wanted to make a difference in people's lives. John said, "I wanted to add value to people. That became the foundation of everything I do." So rather than focusing on the harvest, John began sowing seeds every day. Then, some years later, he decided he wanted to accelerate his sowing efforts and elevated his commitment to "add value to leaders who multiply value to others."[2] But what exactly is required to accomplish that? This goes back to the question John asked the gentleman at the conference, "Would you like to do what I did?"

He and I talked about his Rule of Five—the five things he does every day. He reads, thinks, files, asks questions, and writes. Every day. Of course, these are John's five. You will have to find your own five.

As for executing of the Rule of Five, John shared an analogy about what it takes to chop a tree down: swing five times every day.

1. Know what you want to accomplish. (Cut the tree down.)
2. Get the right tool. (Use an axe. A baseball bat won't work.)
3. Stay focused. (Keep cutting the same tree.)
4. Remain consistent. (Do it every day. You only have to swing five times if you do it every day.)
5. Stay with it until the task is accomplished. (No need to ask how long it takes. You're done when the tree falls.)

What do you want to accomplish? Determine your Rule of Five. This does not come without daily discipline. John knew he couldn't add value to others unless he continued to develop himself.

I asked John what has kept him going for more than fifty years helping people by adding value to their lives, and he quickly responded, "Fruit! Seeing the fruit of growth and success in other people's lives keeps me going." My next question was very candid. "John, you don't really *need* to keep doing all this. You work so hard. So what keeps you in the game at this stage in your life?" He paused, then said, "When you can afford to quit and are highly successful is not the time to quit, because your greatest return is right in front of you."[3] With passion, John added, "Fruit creates the anticipation of more fruit. It's a greater return that creates anticipation and that's what gets me up at 5:30 a.m. every day, because I anticipate fruit."[4]

Daily discipline is critical and serves as the foundation, but results will always beat discipline over the long haul. John stated with confidence, "You can be very disciplined, but without fruit you'll give up after a while. That's why you need to know your top five—your essentials. You'll know you have the right essentials when your work delivers fruit."[5]

> "Seeing the fruit of growth and success in other people's lives keeps me going."
> —JOHN MAXWELL

My last question during our interview was, "John, how do you describe your confidence as a leader?" He was hesitant to share, but finally said, "I've always been a confident person. I'm comfortable in my own skin, I know who I am. Confidence in my life is a gift, and I've accepted it. I just can't take credit for a gift."[6]

You will likely find the third and final part of this book the most practical. Now that we have addressed the foundational decisions and character development, it's time to focus on the leadership competencies that will strengthen your confidence in the most practical ways. They are the leadership practices you do every day: determine direction, focus on the game plan, care about those you lead, communicate an optimistic message, and develop leaders.

CHAPTER 11

DIRECTION

KNOW WHERE YOU ARE GOING AND LEADING OTHERS

There is no more powerful engine driving an organization
toward excellence and long-range success than an attractive,
worthwhile and achievable vision of the future, widely shared.
—BURT NANUS

The RMS *Titanic* was in a class of its own. It was a luxury steamship that spared no expense. The most celebrated ship of its time boasted opulent state rooms, a stunning candelabra, an onboard gymnasium, a swimming pool, libraries, an elegant grand staircase, high-class restaurants, a Turkish bath, a squash court, and even an eight-piece orchestra. It was truly magnificent, and, her builders assured, it was absolutely unsinkable.[1]

The passengers included the rich and famous as well as hundreds of ordinary people, families with children, and immigrants who were headed for the United States hopeful for a better life.[2]

The voyage was smooth. The ship ran beautifully. It was truly a marvel of engineering for its day. Harland and Wolff, the builders, had a stellar reputation. Everyone took great pride in the ship's construction and put tremendous confidence in its ability to perform. The *Titanic* seemed invulnerable, yet we all know the end of the story. So what happened?

Work began on the *Titanic* in March 1909 in a shipyard in Belfast, Ireland. She sailed for New York from Southampton, England, on April 10, 1912. After approximately three years of construction, the *Titanic* was at sea for barely five days before its tragic sinking on April 15. It took only two hours and forty minutes to go down after hitting an unexpected iceberg,[3] and more than fifteen hundred souls were lost.[4]

There can be a fine line between confidence and overconfidence, and it is often costly. The *Titanic's* story is more dramatic than most and the results were tragic, but the principle is the same. In any number of examples, from an overzealous church plant project to a large church building campaign, overconfidence can get leaders into costly trouble.

Perhaps one of the greatest leadership errors resulting from overconfidence was made by J. Bruce Ismay, the chairman and managing director of White Star, the shipping line famous for moving cargo and passengers between the British Empire and the United States. Ismay was aboard the *Titanic* for its maiden voyage and ordered the experienced senior captain, Edward Smith, to abandon caution and race to reach New York in record time.[5] The extreme overconfidence also contributed to the gross shortage of lifeboats. The *Titanic* carried a mere sixteen lifeboats plus four Engelhardt "collapsibles" that could accommodate only 1,178 people,[6] when it sailed with approximately 2,224 passengers and crew. Less than half stood a chance, and many lifeboats were launched far under capacity. Sadly, there were only 705 estimated survivors.

> Outcomes matter and leaders are responsible.

There is a great responsibility when it comes to providing direction. Outcomes matter and leaders are responsible. A strong vision and clear direction are required and will greatly strengthen your confidence for the journey ahead.

Vision Sets Direction

Vision is a picture of the preferred future, while direction points the way. When vision moves from the heart of the visionary to the hearts of the people, potential is released. Direction allows the vision to be seen and become real. It allows movement and progress to begin.

Can You Lead Without a Vision?

You may have experienced a time in your leadership where the vision wasn't clear, and you didn't know what was next and new for your church. That's not an uncommon experience, but the outcome is determined by how you handle the tension.

Some leaders panic and others pause. They pause to pray, reflect, seek God, and gain insight from a few trusted leaders. Those leaders who panic try to manufacture a vision. That never works and deflates their confidence.

Can you still lead when you don't have a current vision? Yes. But not indefinitely. The best way to lead when without a vision is to focus on the Great Commission (Matthew 28:19–20) and make that your clear and inspiring battle cry. Allow your emphasis on it to lead you to a new vision.

The Birth of a Vision

Is it your dream or God's plan? Candidly, that's not always easy to discern, but the difference is critically important. Ultimately, your dream and God's plan should match (Psalm 37:4). "Make disciples of all nations" (Matthew 28:19) is the right biblical place to start. That is the mission, God's purpose, and the foundation of your vision, which makes that mission personal to you and your church. Vision is the fire, fuel, and flavor that makes your church and its culture special. The mission is universal; the vision is unique.

Vision begins with a burden. The story of Nehemiah is a great example. Remember the heartache when the men from Judah said to Nehemiah, "'Those who survived the exile and are back in the province are in great trouble and disgrace. The wall of Jerusalem is broken down, and its gates have been burned with fire.' When I heard these things, I sat down and wept. For some days I mourned and fasted and prayed before the God of heaven" (Nehemiah 1:3–4).

We'll return to Nehemiah, but for now, what is your burden? What concern or problem weighs on your heart and compels you to action? The answer to that question is the beginning of your vision.

> **Vision begins with a burden.**

Four Ways to Developing a Great Vision

1. Vision Draws People Toward the Future

Two of the most legitimate fears of a leader are to either drift or get stuck. Without intentionality, all churches naturally drift toward what is comfortable, rather than pressing forward toward the new and next. Even the busyness of ministry can cause you to drift to the side or, in some cases, backward.

A prolonged drift leads to getting stuck. The remedy is a strong vision that compels you to drive forward no matter how difficult, costly, or long it takes. Truly leading forward is like running directly into a strong wind. It's hard, and it would be so much easier to head in a direction of less resistance. But any easy option will pull you away from your vision, and when you are off course, your confidence gets derailed.

> It's essential that your vision carries a sense of a better future.

With this in mind, your vision, whether for a student ministry, small group, or the entire church, must be compelling enough to inspire the people to forward movement. Therefore, it's essential that your vision carries a sense of a better future, one in which the people see value and want to be a part of it.

2. Vision Unites the People

The people in a group or organization of any size, large or small, naturally want to go their own way. It's usually not out of rebellion or just to be difficult. It's most often because people have their own opinions, preferences, and ideas. It's what makes people unique, and the means by which they add value. But unique and valuable or not, without alignment, vision will not work. There must be unity among the people to head in a unified direction together. When your congregation is unified, the people can achieve far more together than even the most powerful few people can on their own.

A few years ago, the 12Stone congregation made a commitment to help improve both the spiritual and physical well-being of the poor, restoring their dignity, purpose, and freedom. The tangible aspect was to dig wells for fresh water. The direction was clear, and the vision was strong. We would provide fresh water to change lives in Kenya and Haiti. People would no longer need to walk daily for hours to get dirty and contaminated water. A well in a village not only brings life-giving clean water but it also makes room for education, economic development, and church advancement.

Partnering with 410 Bridge, the 12Stone congregation contributed more than $1.1 million to this vision. More than 59 wells or access points to fresh water have been completed, ultimately affecting more than 160,000 people. And more than 600 of our 12Stoners have traveled to one of the two countries. This would never have been possible without unity because it took all of us working together and pooling our resources to make a difference.

3. Vision Creates Momentum

As I discussed more thoroughly in chapter 8, change is necessary, yet everyone resists change to some degree. It takes momentum to break through to the new and next on both a personal level for you as a leader and for the congregation. Vision creates that momentum.

Your vision must be large enough to create enthusiasm but not so large that it seems completely out of reach. If your congregation has been hurt, lacks trust, or hasn't experienced a "win" in a long time, your large vision may

> A small wind will still move the boat!

need to start smaller—in bite-size phases—and build over time. Never despise a little momentum. A small wind will still move the boat! It's far more important to move forward than to overreach and stall. Your vision needs to be big enough to need God, but not so big that it becomes a burden on the people.

4. Vision Inspires the Best in People

You know when your vision has been developed well because it inspires people. They rise above their own needs and concerns to join and participate in something bigger than they are. They are also willing to sacrifice time and resources to see the vision become a reality. Money follows vision and clear direction, and vision inspires generosity.

I've watched the Live Sent vision catch deep traction at 12Stone Church. As God sent Jesus into the world, he sent us into the world (John 17:18). Live Sent has inspired thousands of people to move from their comfort zones to reach people with compassion, practical help, and the gospel. From buying a meal for the car behind them in a fast-food drive-through to helping a single mom put tires on her car, people have engaged the vision Pastor Kevin Myers casted.

Stories abound, from people driving daily to a hospital to comfort someone suffering from cancer surgery or a stroke to giving a couple facing divorce hope for their marriage. A successful vision brings out the best in people and raises their confidence, not only among leaders but the whole congregation.

Four Ways to Build Strategy

1. Build Your Team to Achieve the Goal

Patti and I were at dinner with several friends, and we all talked about taking a vacation cruise together. What a great idea! A fun, relaxing, interesting cruise with people we loved. Except that nothing ever happened. Why? There was no plan. I remember us saying, "I hope we do this." But hope is not a strategy. A worthwhile idea requires a plan, but we didn't have one. And while this was a very capable group, we didn't pick a leader and organize a team either.

The same is true in your church. Until you move your vision from a dream to a measurable strategy, it will remain nothing more than a dream. Some church staffs function more like friends out to dinner with great ideas than a team that can get something done.

Do you have the right mix on your staff (paid or volunteer) to make things happen and get things done? If you are all idea people with no one to focus on strategy and execution, you won't move forward. If you are all strategists but lack a vision that catches traction, you'll be organized but go no further than the visionaries. You need both elements and the ability to work together in productive harmony to move forward.

2. Progress Requires a Strategic Plan

If you're traveling from New York City to Dallas by car and need to arrive in three days, you'll need a clear and measurable plan. Without that plan, no one believes you will get there on time. The same principle is true for your church. Strategy makes progress believable.

Vison unites the team and strategy aligns the team. Alignment is the process by which the leaders and the people come together in agreement about how they will realize the vision. The vision represents the why, and the strategy encompasses the what and how. As discussed in the previous section, the vision unites people together, but without alignment that sense of enthusiasm will soon fade. Alignment refines and brings focus to the vision, which sets the stage for a successful strategic plan.

> **The plan must never overshadow the vision, and the vision must respect the plan.**

The plan must never overshadow the vision, and the vision must respect the plan. The two come together and become effective by agreed upon goals and the measurement of those goals. As you construct a strategy, here are seven key questions to answer:

- Who is the point leader?
- Who is on the lead team? (You will need the right mix of skill sets and experience to cover the pertinent issues.)
- How are decisions made?
- What are the key objectives and the preferred timeline?
- What are the obstacles in your path?
- What resources are required?
- How will you review and measure progress and determine success?

Your plan needs to be simple enough to fit on two or three pages, yet thorough enough to acknowledge the scope and reality of what is before you.

3. Disciplined Diligence Is Necessary for Execution

Your strategy is only as good as your commitment to see it through to completion. One church expert said it this way:

- Failing churches make no plans.
- Average churches make plans but falter in commitment to execute them.
- Good churches make plans and intermittently stick to them.
- Great churches make plans and execute them to completion.

The primary difference between good and great is disciplined diligence. Discipline deals with your inner character. Do you have the right stuff? Diligence deals with your outward focus. Are you doing the right things?

You will drift from your strategy if you are not disciplined in who you are (vision, values, and culture) and diligent in what you do. Without discipline you will drift toward comfortable relationships and leadership that doesn't stretch you. Without diligence you will drift toward an inward focus, discipleship over evangelism, and maintenance over progress.

4. A Successful System for Decision Making Is Mandatory

Nothing ruins a great strategy faster than getting stuck in the mire of a muddy system for making decisions. How are decisions made at your church? It's not so much about the "right way," as it is about a system that's clear and works for you, guided by the Holy Spirit. A good four-step structure to build upon is data, debate, decision, or defer.[7] Base all decisions on facts, not on emotion or opinion. Discuss and debate the data, then either make a decision or defer with good reason. You will not always agree with each other, but once the decision is made, stick together like your lives depend on it.

A great tool to strengthen your team's ability to handle decision-making tension is the "project management triangle."[8] It's based on the three facets of time, money, and quality. It helps you wrestle the complexities of scope, constraints, and value, and goes like this: you can have two out of three, but you can't have all three.

- You can have it fast and inexpensive, but the quality will be less than you desire.
- You can have it fast and high quality, but you will pay a premium.
- You can have it inexpensive and high quality, but it will take an extremely long time.

This helpful tool can easily be adapted to nearly any strategy for a vision or project at your church.

Nehemiah: The Strategic Leader

I've always loved the story of Nehemiah. As a leader, he was a strategic thinker and also had a heart of compassion. Like Moses and David, God worked through Nehemiah in a purposeful way that provided the clear direction he needed to gain confidence for the difficulties that were to come.

Nehemiah was born to Jewish parents in Persia during their long exile from Jerusalem. He was appointed as cupbearer to Artaxerxes, king of Persia. The position of cupbearer was highly trusted, influential, and allowed Nehemiah a close and confidential connection with the king. This special role included tasting the king's drinks in case they contained poison.

Upon hearing Nehemiah's distress for the city of Jerusalem, Artaxerxes appointed him governor and provided resources to rebuild the wall and restore God's people from their brokenness to a place of renewed confidence and faith. Nehemiah's leadership and discipline would prove invaluable in this complex process. The remaining five chapters will unfold the narrative of Nehemiah's life and leadership.

NEHEMIAH'S BURDEN

"While I [Nehemiah] was in the citadel of Susa, . . . one of my brothers came from Judah with some other men, and I questioned them about the Jewish remnant that had survived the exile, and also about Jerusalem. They said to me, 'Those who survived the exile and are back in the province are in great trouble and disgrace. The wall of Jerusalem is broken down, and its gates have been burned with fire.' When I heard these things, I sat down and wept" (Nehemiah 1:1–4).

The report from his brother hit Nehemiah like a ton of fallen bricks. Knowledge of his brethren living under duress, imagining the collapsed wall of Jerusalem, the shocking awareness of the reality of Israel's lost glory—all of it conspired to conjure up images of devastation and ruin that weighed on Nehemiah like a burden on his very soul.

The Jewish people had suffered a tremendous setback. And they remained defeated. They needed to bounce back, but how? A foundational key to resilience is hope. Without it, resilience is impossible. And a specific vision—a direction for the future—is the only source for such a hope.

"Why does your face look so sad? . . . This can be nothing but sadness of heart," King Artaxerxes asked him (Nehemiah 2:2). "What is it you want?" (Nehemiah 2:4). Nehemiah was afraid. As a mere servant of the king, he had no right to ask the king for anything. What he did have, though, was a mind burdened by images of ruins and broken people. This negative vision required the birthing of a positive one to counteract it.

Nehemiah cast his vision to his king. "If your servant has found favor in [the king's] sight . . . send me to the city in Judah where my ancestors are buried so that I can rebuild it" (Nehemiah 2:5).

The king, moved by Nehemiah's heart, agreed. He then asked specific questions about when he would go and how long it would take. In other words, he began asking about strategy, because without a plan a vision cannot come to be. Nehemiah next proved why the king trusted him. He was no simpleton. After laying out a time frame, he began detailing his needs and requesting letters from the king to certain officials to obtain the building materials he would need and for safe passage. A strategy was already in place. This clear direction and strategy gave Nehemiah the confidence to ask the king for help, and those same things gave the king confidence in Nehemiah to execute it.

Like Nehemiah, we all experience the need for vision, direction, and strategy. The moment we move from the planning phase to the realities of opposition, complications, and tough times, leadership becomes much more complex. This is not unlike Jenni's story.

> Like Nehemiah, we all experience the need for vision, direction, and strategy.

A Conversation with Jenni Catron

How does a young girl, born in a small midwestern, blue-collar town where the snow drifts are often taller than she is, end up first as a record label executive and then as the respected executive pastor of a megachurch?

Jenni Catron grew up in Rhinelander, Wisconsin, under the care of very young and hardworking parents. With a strong desire to go to college and a deep passion for the music business, she began to dream at a very early age about how to get from Rhinelander to Nashville. A genuine music lover, Jenni had studied voice and piano for years. Yet she admits that while her talent was good, it never quite reached the "great" level. The music industry, however, would prove to be the perfect arena to capture her developing gifts of leadership and administration.

After college, Jenni landed her first job at ForeFront Records. She received great leadership and training, and, over the course of a decade, rose to the level of brand manager and artist development director. As a young and gifted leader, Jenni was rocketing toward her dream job as CEO of a major record label.

Then God suddenly interrupted her through an invitation from her pastor to join his staff at the church where Jenni and her husband served.

Torn between God's prompting and love for her job, she decided to take enough time to do some deep soul searching. Jenni had always shown a strong talent for helping team members identify their skills and gifts and then aligning them in the best ways to accomplish their goals. During her soul searching, God made it clear he wanted her to use her talent for his purposes within the church.

Jenni joined the staff at Cross Point Church in Nashville as their executive director in 2005. Jumping into the middle of a rapidly growing church can be like diving into the deep end of a pool where you can't see the edges, but she took on the challenge with enthusiasm and confidence.

In 2010, Nashville was devastated by a flood. Hundreds of Cross Point families were displaced and lost everything. The staff was swiftly consumed with navigating the overwhelming demands of flood relief for the congregation they loved. The pressure was high, and the giving dropped dramatically for two reasons. First, like everyone else in the nation, Nashville had been hit by the severe recession two years earlier in 2008. Second, out of compassion, many in the congregation were redirecting their tithes to neighbors and friends who had also lost everything.

Setting clear direction for the church became extremely difficult. There were more options and opportunities for ministry than ever before, but fewer resources than ever. As you might imagine, there was no shortage of opinions, passion, and an equal amount of questions about what to do to establish a direction and clear strategy.

Leading the staff through this difficult decision-making process went to the core of Jenni's job. As the staff was physically navigating flood relief, they were experiencing emotional fatigue, and, for the first time ever, possibly some job cuts. On top of this, three of their staff members had also lost their homes to the flood.

How could Jenni, along with the senior pastor, elders, and executive team, save everyone's jobs? How could she help hold the team together and maintain morale while leading them through this very real disaster? To say the least, emotions ran high, and tough decisions were required of Jenni.

Somehow, they made it through the turbulence without any staff cuts. I asked Jenni how her confidence had weathered that storm. She said, "The right decisions weren't always obvious, and some were difficult for the staff to understand. But ultimately, surviving that season forged the confidence I needed to make the right decisions, even though they weren't popular. I had my doubts and insecurities, but during that season I *had* to be confident."[9]

She also explained how the board of directors' unwavering support of her then was also a key help in boosting her leadership confidence. Jenni described her overall leadership confidence as a roller coaster of sorts that ultimately produced what she calls a "humble confidence."[10]

She clarifies that by saying, "Sometimes my confidence paralleled my identity found in my work, which wasn't always good. If I was given a role, title, and responsibility, along with the trust from those above me, and I added to that my desire to achieve, my confidence was strong. But when a new challenge came along, my confidence could easily drop if it wasn't rooted in God. When confidence comes from competence it is often accompanied by arrogance. When confidence comes from a true centeredness in God—knowing my gifts and opportunities come from him—my confidence is covered by humility."[11]

Jenni went on to be the executive pastor at Menlo Church, in Menlo Park, California, and is now the founder and CEO of the 4Sight Group, where she is a focused author, speaker, and coach.

And focus is the subject of our next chapter.

CHAPTER 12

FOCUS

STICK TO THE GAME PLAN

*I don't care how much power, brilliance or energy
you have. If you don't harness it and focus it on a
specific target and hold it there, you're never going
to accomplish as much as your ability warrants.*

—ZIG ZIGLAR

The sun is a powerful source of energy. Every hour the sun washes the earth with billions of kilowatts of energy. Yet with a hat and some sunscreen you can bathe in the light of the sun for hours at a time with few ill effects.

"A laser is a weak source of energy. A laser takes a few watts of energy and focuses them in a coherent stream of light. But with a laser you can drill a hole in a diamond or wipe out a cancer."[1]

Your church or business operates in the same way. The more focused you are, the greater impact you make. The challenge is, each person we serve is an individual and therefore unique in his or her desires, needs, and preferences. Because of this, we often attempt to launch more ministries in order to reach more people, but this often results in reaching fewer people. It takes discipline and focus to reach more people.

"In the physical world, unfocusing is called entropy, or disorder. And Rudolf Clausius's law of entropy states that over time, the entropy of any closed system increases. Let's say you straighten out your clothes closet. A month later, the closet is a mess. You have witnessed the effects of entropy, one of the fundamental laws of nature."[2]

In this respect, churches are no different from clothes closets. Over time every church tends to become unfocused. Diversification may work well for your retirement account, but it's not a good approach for your church. It's like multitasking, a once touted principle now being debunked and refuted on a regular basis. Focus rules.

> Over time every church tends to become unfocused.

Take, for example, multiple styles of worship services at one church. This approach is not *wrong*, but the question is, does it deliver the greatest impact of your resources to the greatest number of people? I've attended churches that offered a traditional service at 8:30 a.m., a contemporary service at 10:00 a.m., and finally, a "for singles and young adults only" at 11:30 a.m. That's a massive amount of effort and energy to reach just a few more people. Is one more person worth it? In terms of eternity, yes, of course. Yet when you also consider the lives of your staff, the time of your volunteers, and the effect of your resources, it does beg a few more questions, such as, What if by simply casting vision differently, those same people would attend a service that's for everyone?

Perhaps God made it clear that he wants multiple styles of worship in your church. If so, that's good, you should go for it. But short of that, the principle of focus is nearly always in your favor.

Consider your approach to local outreach. Which has a deeper community influence? A few thousand dollars each to many local partners or focusing your resources on a few key initiatives connected with strategic partners? The power of focus combined with partnerships is tremendous and yields incredible kingdom results.

The larger a church becomes and the longer it exists, the greater the demand for more ministries. When this pressure is put on the leadership and they add those ministries, it nearly always results in diminishing results because you simply can't do everything well. Therefore, a focused ministry that yields sustained high impact requires great effort from focused leaders. A leader who does this well is Pastor Chris Hodges.

A Conversation with Chris Hodges

How does a leader build a church of more than fifty thousand in regular weekend attendance? Is the discipline of focus a big part of the answer? How does confidence fit into the equation?

Chris Hodges was born in Baton Rouge, Louisiana, and raised by godly parents. His mom's love was nurturing, and his dad's influence was impactful. Chris's father was an auditor by profession and had a brilliant accounting mind. He was precise, disciplined, and meticulous about everything in a life-giving way. Excellence mattered. This made a profound imprint on Chris as a child. It's no wonder that his favorite subject in school was math, and that he pursued business in college.

God interrupted Chris's plan with an invitation to participate in a ministry internship at age nineteen with Bethany Church, helping to lead camps and mission trips for students. By 1984, Chris was in full-time ministry and a full-time college student.

The next opportunity for ministry came in Colorado Springs, Colorado, with a church plant. Chris served as worship leader, youth pastor, and even senior associate pastor, which gave him the opportunity to teach in a formal capacity regularly. In 1994, Chris and his wife, Tammy, returned to Bethany as a cell group district pastor.

The door to his destiny opened seven years later in 2001, when Chris planted Church of the Highlands in Birmingham, Alabama. That church now averages more than fifty thousand people a weekend. Chris gives much of the credit for this success to what he calls the "Dream Team," but recognizes that obviously his leadership played a key role as well.

I asked Chris how his upbringing influenced his leadership and he said, "My discipline, routine, and focus is not based on legalism, it's based on the value I saw coming from it. There is freedom in focus."[3]

When I asked about the focus of his church, he responded, "My early spiritual development marked me with mission and the Great Commission—to win the lost. That's all there is. It's the responsibility of the church and there is no other purpose. We don't get distracted with anything else."[4]

The fourfold focus of Church of the Highlands is:

1. *Evangelism.* Preaching salvation in Jesus.
2. *Pastoral.* Helping people grow through brokenness to begin the process of regeneration, deliverance, and healing.
3. *Training and discipleship.* Learning your God-given purpose and growing into the person God wants you to be.
4. *Mobilization.* Being sent into the world to live out your faith. Chris shared with passion, "I wake up every day thinking and dreaming about how to do this and do it better."[5]

A big aha moment in this conversation was when Pastor Chris said, "If I have brought anything to the church it is a crazy focus on making our process crystal clear and easy to understand—especially to something that can often become complicated and unclear. Our focus on precise language brought clarity and the church really took off."[6]

> "Our focus on precise language brought clarity and the church really took off."
> —CHRIS HODGES

In 2018, Church of the Highlands had more than sixty thousand in small groups, more than thirty-three thousand salvations, and twenty-three thousand actively serving on the Dream Team. Focus seems to matter. As they have continued to grow, their focus has remained intact. With their resources, Church of the Highlands could do more, but they've intentionally remained fiercely focused and kept their mission clear and simple.

When I asked Chris to describe his confidence as a leader, he responded, "My confidence comes from my relationships. I'm blessed, I know, but I'm a very secure person. I know what God thinks of me, I know what my father thought of me, and I know what my family, mentors, and close friends think. True confidence is based on knowing who you are. I know who I am, and I'm not derailed by others' thoughts. This close inner circle is enough, and my confidence is strong."[7] I've always appreciated the humble, yet confident authenticity that oozes out of Pastor Chris. He's a brilliant leader and a great visionary, and he is passionate about reaching people for Jesus.

The next thought that Pastor Chris shared is a profoundly helpful insight to confidence: "There are only two times in the Bible when God the Father spoke directly to the Son. First, at Jesus' baptism, and second, at the Mount of Transfiguration. Both times God said the same thing. This is my Son (accepted), whom I love (affection), with him I'm well pleased (affirmation). With those three things: acceptance, affection, and affirmation, God ushered Jesus into ministry with confidence."[8]

Chris's insight was powerful and, yet, even Jesus faced distraction. Jesus was led by the Spirit into the wilderness and was tempted and tested by Satan (Luke 4:1–13). In many ways, these three tests were an intentional distraction, attempting to pull Jesus from his priorities of the Word, worship, and focus on doing the Father's will. You and I also face temptations, often in the form of distractions, and when they work, our confidence takes a hit.

Overcoming Distraction

Distraction is a chief enemy of every leader. Daily distractions pull you away from your key responsibilities and top priorities. It takes daily discipline to remain focused.

People, projects, and problems clamor for your time, but no matter how much you may want to help, you can't say yes to everything and everyone. The ability to discern the difference between a distraction that derails you and a divine interruption that needs you, therefore, is a key leadership skill.

Someone may stop by during your day or call you on the phone, indicating God has a special encounter in mind. But it could also be a waste of time. How do you know the difference? Discernment is a big part of leadership. Ask the Holy Spirit for guidance in the moment. Knowing how to focus on the right things at the right times is essential. Without intentional focus, your progress and overall effectiveness decreases, and your confidence drops as well.

There are, of course, the distractions that we bring on ourselves. One of mine is email. I'm a type-A person and pride myself on being pretty fast at handling emails. I find myself thinking, *Well, I am going to respond to*

> **Some things just don't need to be done at all.**

this email at some point, so why not just knock it out now? None of my mentors would be thrilled with that approach, because it's allowing someone else's priority to take me off my own priorities and lose focus. The truth is that emptying my in-box is easier than doing some of my more complex thought work, and it provides quick gratification. It's a shiny distraction that gets my attention.

That doesn't mean I don't care about the email request or don't want to help. I do. It means I need to focus on the right things at the right times. And some things just don't need to be done at all.

One of the first steps in learning to overcome the constant temptation of distraction is to know what common distractions look like, so you can proactively be on the lookout. If you know what's coming, you have a better chance to resist them. Make a list of the things that typically distract you. For me it's things like great opportunities, worry (yes, a complete waste of time), and the ever-present email.

A Three-Step Plan to Increase Your Focus

1. Set Your Direction

Focus starts with the big picture not the details. If you don't know where you're going, you'll never be focused. It's like trying to put a thousand-piece puzzle together without the picture on the box cover.

What is your vision? Where is your church headed? Where do you want to go? You can't get there if you chase multiple big goals. I love the quote that says, "If you chase two rabbits you catch neither."[9] Pick a rabbit!

Maybe you're not the senior pastor; perhaps you are the student pastor or a volunteer small-group leader. The question is still relevant. Where are you going? Where are you leading your group? You can't do everything, so choose wisely and focus.

2. Commit to Your Decision

It's not uncommon for a church, or a specific ministry within the church, to set a direction but then change their mind in a short time. Changing your mind is not the problem unless it's a habit. Sometimes you need to change directions. Adaptability, as we have previously discussed, is an important ability. But changing your mind before you've actually worked the plan is a problem.

Here's a typical scenario: You set the direction, but it doesn't go as easily as you thought. You hit some speed bumps and experience a setback. Then you receive some advice or attend a conference where a leader tells you about how their church grew by leaps and bounds. You are inspired, and his or her vision and plan sounds as if it will work better than yours, so you change your mind and your direction. The problem is that you didn't focus on your plan long enough to know if it will really work.

The truth is, most of the time it's not the vision, direction, or even the plan that's the problem, but the leader's lack of ability to stick with the plan day after day and make it work. Allow me to be blunt: sometimes distractions are more fun than the daily grind to get the job done.

Making a decision, however, is about commitment. Your vision and direction are probably good. Stay focused and watch your effectiveness rise, and your confidence will rise with it.

3. Leverage Your Drive and Discipline

Once you know where you're going and you've made the commitment to stick with it, you still need the daily drive and discipline to arrive at your destination.

Your personal drive as a leader comes from your passion. Remaining focused on something you don't care about is difficult, so it has to matter to you. You need to genuinely care enough to say no to other things in order to stay focused on your commitments and priorities. Your internal drive is like the engine of a car, and the fuel is your passion. Discipline is the ability to stay on the road and not get distracted with side roads that take you off course.

> Your personal drive as a leader comes from your passion.

Daily discipline doesn't suggest mechanical drudgery. You need time to rest, play, work on your new and improved ministry, and be creative. You can do all that while staying focused on what you want to accomplish. In fact, use your creative side to dream how to improve your current plan and focus on it, not drop it to chase another rabbit.

Once you develop your personal discipline of focus, you can then leverage that to your organizational discipline of focus. Let me say that again in a slightly different way: your personal discipline of focus as a leader must always come first, or you will jump from strategy to strategy and ministry to ministry.

The Wisdom of Lean

In my thirty-five-plus years of ministry, I've coached and consulted with hundreds of churches. Only a few seem to have narrowed their approach to a focused ministry. By contrast, most have a large and growing menu of what they offer. The heart behind all they provide is generous. However, the strategic use of the energy invested for limited kingdom return could be wisely reconsidered. Let's take a look at why.

It's impossible for one local church to effectively lead every conceivable ministry. Therefore, the critical questions are: How many ministries should your church lead and which ones? How many is too many? How do you decide?

Churches are prone to add ministries while simultaneously they resist eliminating ministries, regardless of their level of effectiveness. That's a recipe for overload and exhaustion. It's why most church leaders are busy to the point of utter fatigue. Yet all that activity doesn't translate to commensurate growth and missional progress.

Why Fewer Ministries than More?

Here's a quick three-point framework to help you think through this concept with your team:

1. When your ministries are allowed to follow their own course, without change or pruning, they will become more complicated and less productive over time.

2. The larger a church becomes, the ratio of energy to results yields decreasing returns. Fewer ministries would allow you to refocus your energy for greater results.

3. The more complex a church becomes, the less the leaders believe simplicity in approach can be achieved. Without intentionality, they may get discouraged or even less focused, and possibly give up.

Margin Is the Key

1. A lean ministry model helps create the margin that allows you to get better at and improve the ministries you do offer. Focused effort on fewer ministries increases the impact of each ministry, and that results in a greater number of changed lives.

2. A lean ministry approach helps create margin for your congregation to pursue God personally and build healthier families. By having fewer ministry programs to attend, families can be at home with more time together. Your congregation, in general, has more time to meet and invite new friends to church.

3. A lean ministry model will help you create the margin that increases your ability to respond to Holy Spirit prompts. Lean ministry does not quell the Holy Spirit, it creates more space for him to move. When you are so busy you can barely catch your breath, it's hard to listen to and respond to God prompts. I'll acknowledge that in most churches that practice a lean model, it doesn't always feel like there is much more time, but that's because they work much harder and deeper at making what they do better. But, in turn, that is how they reach more people. In other words, rather than doing the same things with the same people over and over again, you are more closely connected to the mission of the church to reach more people for Jesus and help them mature in their faith.

The tension will never go away. People are passionate about their chosen ministries, and most of those ministries are good. That's why the decisions are difficult. But, when a well-meaning volunteer decides to change ministries or even leave your church, you now own what he or she started. It won't be long before you end up with way too much to do, much of which is not truly effective. At least not when you compare energy invested to more focused results, measured by life change.

The Divine Thumbprint

If you agree with me that no one church can do everything, then how you decide what ministries you do and how you do them is crucial. The decisions should not be made based on popularity, pressure, size of personality, politics, or emotion.

The best approach is for the lead team to come together in prayer, and then take a spiritually strategic approach. A lean ministry doesn't limit the Spirit of God. The Holy Spirit guides and directs you to the ministries intended for your church in that season. Then he breathes life and power into those chosen ministries.

But you should always design your ministry architecture with a big-picture view, rather than randomly adding ministries as you go. You gain great confidence as a leader when you know your "ministry menu" has been directed by God and thought through as a team.

The principle of the divine thumbprint is that God's plan for your ministries is not random; rather, it's specific and focused. Start by adding no further ministries until you have clear direction. Next, agree on your list of the irreducible minimum. This is your "must have" ministries for the church to operate. Then begin to slowly eliminate ministries, starting with those that are not very effective. Do this sensitively, honoring those who have served those ministries; and remember to communicate well to help those resistant to the change. And finally, slowly and prayerfully add ministries that are not absolutely needed but make your church uniquely you in your community. Overall, the net list of ministries should not slowly creep up in size, because that defeats the purpose of getting lean in the first place.

Finish What You Started

When you learn the art of focus, you'll love the benefits. You can then concentrate on progress. Keep moving forward. Eliminate the nonessentials and resist distractions. Listen for the voice of God and prompts from the Holy Spirit.

> When you learn the art of focus, you'll love the benefits.

All this will free you up and set you up to finish what you started. Perhaps surprisingly, many local church leaders are not good at finishing. Ideas and creativity are in abundance, but accomplishing a predetermined written goal is not as common as we would like. The stories of finishing what you started will inspire you to keep going, like in the story of Nehemiah.

NEHEMIAH'S FOCUS

"It is reported among the nations . . . that you and the Jews are plotting to revolt . . . therefore you are building the wall . . . Now this report will get back to the king; so come, let us meet together" (Nehemiah 6:6–7).

That excerpt was part of a letter from Sanballat the Horonite. Nehemiah read between the lines and knew it was just one more attempt to frighten him.

Sanballat was one of three political governors who had not stopped opposing Nehemiah since he arrived, even though he had a mandate from the king himself to rebuild Jerusalem. Together, the triumvirate controlled the north, east, and south, and essentially surrounded Nehemiah and the returned Judeans. The power structure of Sanballat and the others was directly threatened by Nehemiah's plan, and they weren't planning to roll over and let it happen.

Nehemiah's strategy for seeing his vision come to fruition had a very simple first step: rebuild the broken-down wall around the Old City. In ancient times, armed raids and banditry were commonplace.

So a city without a wall was completely vulnerable. Jerusalem could not thrive without a wall to protect its citizens; therefore, that was Nehemiah's urgent focus.

Upon arriving, Nehemiah surveyed the ruins and told the people, "You see the trouble we are in . . . let us rebuild . . . and we will no longer be in disgrace" (Nehemiah 2:17). The people threw themselves into the task, each family taking responsibility for a different section of construction inspired by their leader's confidence they could accomplish it.

At first, the opposing leaders just ridiculed the effort saying, "Even a fox climbing up on it would break down their wall" (Nehemiah 4:3). Then, rumors began flying that Sanballat was raising an army to attack Nehemiah's people and disrupt their progress. Rather than get distracted, Nehemiah instructed the people to arm themselves: "And each of the builders wore his sword at his side as he worked" (Nehemiah 4:18).

When Sanballat heard they were ready to fight, he tried a different method of distraction. He sent multiple letters demanding Nehemiah meet to talk. Each time, Nehemiah simply replied, "I am carrying on a great project and cannot go down. Why should the work stop while I leave it and go down to you?" (Nehemiah 6:3).

Even in the face of new threats regarding lies of rebellion being communicated to the king, Nehemiah did not let fear distract him. Because of this focus, in less than two months, the people were able to complete a wall that normally would have taken years, and they defeated Sanballat.

Focused effort and energy will get the job done, strengthen your confidence, and perhaps even inspire the people. But it will not necessarily win their hearts. Caring about your people is the focus of our next chapter.

CHAPTER 13

HEART

CARE GENUINELY ABOUT THOSE YOU LEAD

*Great leaders genuinely care for and love the people
they lead more than they love leading itself.*
—RICK WARREN

My mom passed away unexpectedly in 1997. She was sixty-six years old. Betty, to her friends and clients, managed a travel agency most of her adult life and loved to learn. She was taking her first computer course that year. She was out and about on a beautiful San Diego day, driving in her Volvo she loved, and then after an appointment she felt faint and collapsed. Mom had suffered a stroke.

When I received the call, I was sitting in a dentist chair, numbed up, ready for the drilling to begin. As soon as the dentist finished what he was doing, I raced to the hospital. My wife, Patti, was the first on the scene and met the ambulance. Mom was on a ventilator. The doctors tried to offer hope, but hours later a more candid surgeon walked in, showed me the large dark-colored area at the base of her brain, and said, "I'm sorry, but we don't expect her to wake up." That was a devastating moment.

Patti and I left the hospital and drove home, trying to take in what had

You can't fake caring.

just happened. I was still on staff at Skyline Church then, and later that evening my phone rang. It was John.

Hearing his voice in that moment meant the world to me. He was not only my pastor, he was my friend. He was speaking somewhere in the country, but not only did he stop everything to call me, he canceled the rest of what he had planned, flew back to San Diego, and was sitting with us in my living room the next day.

The point of the story is not that you have to get on a plane and fly somewhere to show you care. The point is that you can't fake caring. Genuine love and care come from the heart and require action, and people know when it's real.

This is much like the genuine love and care Pastor Crawford Loritts has for his congregation in Roswell, Georgia.

A Conversation with Dr. Crawford Loritts

Born in Newark, New Jersey, and raised by two incredible Christian parents, Crawford was saved during a church service at thirteen years of age. A hunger for God's Word ignited within him, and he grew quickly in his faith.

Crawford was just sixteen when he preached his first sermon. Laughing, he told me he'd rediscovered his notes from that sermon and there couldn't have been more than about eleven minutes of content at best! Nonetheless, though he was so young, God's call on his life had been clear.

In 1976, Dr. Loritts cofounded Oak Cliff Bible Fellowship with Dr. Tony Evans in Dallas, Texas. They served together for a short time until God called him to join Campus Crusade for Christ in 1978, where he served for the next twenty-seven years, largely in speaking roles, but always with a heart for discipleship.

"I've always been a churchman," he said. "I've always had a deep love for the church. So in 2005, God moved me to Fellowship Bible Church in Roswell, Georgia, to serve as their senior pastor."[1]

Regarding how to continually sustain love and care for the people in a church, Dr. Loritts said, "Ministry is not about the what, it's about the who."[2]

He went on to explain: "It's not about the events and processes. The primary focus of our calling is to shepherd the hearts of our people. God called me to give myself to the people I serve, and my behavior dictates my emotion. Who my congregation becomes is at the center of *why* I do what I do. That gives me joy, which keeps me going.

"I think it's important that I love the people more than I love what I do for the people. If you make ministry about the people, rather than just try to get people to follow a program, your heart for the people is sustained."[3]

> "The Devil is busy."
> —DR. LORITTS

Dr. Loritts confirmed, too, that conflict is part of leadership and the church is not immune. "Sometimes, I make a decision that people are unhappy with, [and] they might even leave the church." With passion, he said, "The Devil doesn't sit back in his lounge chair while we do ministry. The Devil is busy. He likes to stir up conflict, but the Word of God is everything."[4]

As a direct descendent of former slaves from North Carolina, it would be easy for Dr. Loritts to let history's wounds hurt him. Instead, he says that while growing up, he never even stopped to consider whom he would or would not love.

When we are hurt or discouraged, we pray, seek wisdom, and then get up off our knees and get back to work. Don't carry the burden. It's not ours to carry; it's God's to carry.

"Even when it [conflict] seems personal, like when someone leaves the church over an issue of race, it stings. Our church is about 74 percent white and 26 percent African American, and what I've learned is that the Gospel transcends color. That means love transcends color as well.[5]

"My confidence can take a hit in those moments. It can make me second-guess my decision or wonder if there was something I could have done better, especially if the person has been part of the church for a while. Those things can rattle you. But I've learned to love people through it and hold them with open hands."[6]

I asked Dr. Lorrits to describe his confidence as a leader. He said, "My confidence first grew when I was eighteen years old and was elected president of my class. I didn't seek the office, they put my name forward."[7]

He continued, "Whenever God has wanted me to be somewhere or do something, he's always come and gotten me. I did nothing to deserve any of my blessings in ministry. God orchestrates all of it. That's the key to my confidence. God directs me."[8]

In closing, Dr. Loritts shared this powerful story: "Many years ago, Dr. Bright of Cru, formerly named Campus Crusade for Christ, invited me to speak at a major donor event in Hawaii. Those who attended were impressive people and I was intimidated. I felt like I didn't belong. I was jet-lagged when I arrived and couldn't sleep, so I got up and went for a walk. I told God 'I don't belong here.'

"I'll never forget what he said to me in that moment: 'Crawford, I called you to be here, why do you insult me? With my call comes dignity and confidence.'"[9]

Anyone who knows Crawford Loritts knows he's a presence—a leader with authentic confidence. Charismatic, positive, and upbeat, he is in high demand to speak all over the world. Yet, through it all, he has remained approachable and kind, and it's clear he cares about and loves his congregation.

Caring About People Isn't Automatic

Have you ever gone out to dinner and in just a few minutes discovered that the waiter didn't appear to care? Or perhaps you have worked for a boss who seemed to care more about the project deadline than about you. Maybe you've had a professor or doctor or car mechanic who went through the motions but didn't communicate that they cared. Caring about people is not automatic. It may be more natural for some, but it requires intentionality and effort from any leader who loves the people he or she leads.

One evening I was sitting in a church board meeting, and we were listening to the pastor talk about evangelism. He shared from his heart about lost souls and caring for our neighbors. One board member interrupted with something raw, real, and straight from his heart. The essence was, "I don't really care about my neighbors, at least not enough to move me to action, but I want to." What an incredibly honest statement.

The board member's candid and courageous admission broke him right in that moment. He had been praying that God would give him a heart of genuine love and concern, and that night, God answered his prayer. That honesty and authenticity caught fire among other board members, and then among leaders of the church. A movement swept across the church resulting in tremendous outreach, evangelism, and hundreds saying yes to Jesus. God used a business executive who wasn't sure he cared about his neighbors to start a revival in a local church.

If you don't love others like you want to or feel you should, God can teach you to get there through his Word and prompts from the Holy Spirit. If you don't care about others as deeply as you want to, God will place that emotion within you if you ask him.

Leading people and loving people are closely connected. If your intent is to always do something good or something helpful, even if it doesn't always work out well, you're still doing the right thing. Your motives are good. That kind of internal freedom to make mistakes and learn from them increases your confidence.

Do You Need People or Feed People?

Confident leaders are freed up internally to give themselves away for the good of others. The strength and maturity within you that enables you to focus more on others than yourself is the same strength that increases your confidence as a leader. Like I said in the previous paragraph, you are doing the right thing. Your soul knows it, and you therefore lead better.

A young senior pastor asked me for counsel about his vision casting. We were in a coaching relationship, so I knew he was leading a church of about four hundred people. I watched his sermon online and immediately noticed it appeared he wasn't casting his vision but testing his vision. He wasn't feeding the people by delivering a vision with confidence. He needed the people, so he could find his vision and test it out.

Another leader demonstrated a similar characteristic but with a different twist. In this situation, the pastor was searching to discover who he really was as a leader. He needed the people to confirm and affirm his identity. Each sermon was an attempt to try out a different style, persona, and approach, in order to find out what worked best. An element of that is good. Trying new approaches is part of how we improve, but that's more about practicing communication skills, not becoming who you are as a person and a leader.

This young leader's insecurities were evident; his need for people far outweighed his ability to feed people. He craved hearing, "Good sermon, pastor," more than he desired meeting the spiritual needs of the congregation. Don't jump to conclusions. This pastor was smart, capable, and caring. He just had not yet gotten out of his own way, so he could feed the people more than need them.

Pastor Kevin Myers, at 12Stone Church, says it this way: "It's important to want more *for* the people than *from* them." People can sense when a leader is desperate. Desperation can cause you to lead differently, preach differently, and interact with people differently. For example, if you're under financial

> Desperate leaders are never confident leaders.

pressure, you may be tempted to preach from a place of desperation. In this situation, you want more *from* the people than *for* them. It demonstrates that you need their financial support more than you want their spiritual growth. This can be true in a number of things, from serving relationships to personal friendship. This is rarely if ever intentional, but pressure can have a strong effect, even on good and godly leaders. Desperate leaders are never confident leaders.

Encouragement Lifts People to a Higher Place

I was out for my daily jog and, candidly, I was dragging just a little. I came up around the corner and an elderly gentleman with a winning smile and encouraging tone called out to me as I passed by, "That's some fine steppin' you've got going on there!" That was it. He kept going and I kept jogging. But something changed in that moment. The words "fine steppin' you've got going on there," started ringing in my head and I thought to myself, *You know, I do!* My pace increased, my knees kicked up a little higher, and I was smiling. I no longer cared that young moms pushing baby strollers were flying right by me, because I was steppin' fine!

Encouragement nurtures the soul and fuels the mind. Everyone you lead needs it. A significant element of your role as a leader is to give people hope, build them up, and help them believe in themselves to a greater measure than they have before. In short, your job is to help them live better lives through Christ. Do you see yourself as an encourager in that way? Do others see you as an encouraging leader? yes

Encouragement isn't something you do in a mechanical way. It's not something to check off your list upon completion. It's a way of life for a good leader. Encouragement is not a soft expression from a weak leader. Good leaders are strong leaders who understand that encouragement is a core element to sustained influence. Greater influence leads to better leadership, and your confidence rises because of it.

Essentially, sincere and consistent encouragement comes from a deep love for people and the fact that you genuinely care about them and desire to see them experience life in a better way.

Expressing a Shepherd's Heart in a Rancher's World

It can be tough just to love and care for your own family, let alone an entire congregation. I mean, really, how does that work? How do you express your genuine care to one hundred or three hundred or three thousand people?

Leading through layers takes leadership from the basics to an advanced level. Many of us start out leading by sight. That means your church, campus, or ministry department is small enough that you can simply look around and know who's there and who isn't. You know who's new and who the regulars are. You know the faithful leaders and the troublemakers. You know the prayer warriors and the complainers. You can see them.

When your church gets larger, you learn to lead through layers. That means you raise up and develop other leaders who also lead leaders themselves. Just as an illustration, you might personally lead ten leaders and they each lead eight leaders, for a total of eighty leaders. You can see how fast that can multiply. Does that idea work in terms of love and care? Yes. You love, care about, and shepherd your leaders on a personal level, and those leaders do the same.

There are some additional elements to leading by layers. First, your prayer life includes the full scope of people you are responsible for. Prayer is one of the greatest gifts you can give someone you care about, and you can pray for everyone as a body of believers. Second, when you teach, cast vision, or lead a group of any size, always ask God for a compassionate heart. God modeled that through Jesus, and we are called to possess the same heart. Third, make yourself available to individuals outside your immediate scope of responsibility. Listen for the voice of the Holy Spirit prompting you to show love and care to strangers, people in your church you've never met, and people in need. Do for one what you would like to do for many.

> Do for one what you would like to do for many.

Let's make the distinction with the picture of a shepherd and a rancher. The shepherd directly tends his flock as he sees and cares for each sheep. A rancher leads through ranch hands and handles multiple levels of complexity.

As we return to the narrative on Nehemiah, his heart for the people is evident, even in the complexity of his leadership. Notice the connection between heart and confidence.

NEHEMIAH'S HEART

"Now the men and their wives raised a great outcry against their fellow Jews . . . saying, 'We are mortgaging our fields, our vineyards and our homes to get grain during the famine.' . . . 'We have had to borrow money to pay the king's tax on our fields and vineyards . . . [and] we have to subject our sons and daughters to slavery. Some of our daughters have already been enslaved, but we are powerless'" (Nehemiah 5:1–5).

In the midst of leading the effort to rebuild Jerusalem's wall, Nehemiah was confronted with an ugly truth: that many other Jewish leaders did not share the same heart for the people as he did.

He and others who had returned from Persia had been stretching themselves financially, actively paying local Gentile lords to redeem poor Jews from slavery (Nehemiah 5:8). However, he was learning that, behind the scenes, Jewish nobles had been working directly against their effort, lending money at exorbitant interest rates to the same poor in order to re-enslave them.

Almost assuredly, God's law would have echoed in Nehemiah's mind. "If you lend money to one of my people among you who is needy . . . When they cry out to Me, I will hear, for I [God] am compassionate" (Exodus 22:25, 27).

Injustice naturally infuriates any leader with heart, and Nehemiah was no exception. He says, "When I heard their outcry and these charges, I was very angry" (Nehemiah 5:6). Nehemiah swiftly summoned all the nobles and government officials and accused them of the scheme to their faces.

Only great confidence gave Nehemiah the courage to do this. Insecure rulers are typically consumed by concerns of popularity among their nobles and officials rather than the poor. Nobles are the ones who guarantee their power base, not ordinary farmers with no money.

Nehemiah's heart for his people is what gave him the confidence to confront the elites who considered themselves beyond reproach simply due to their status. From God's law, Nehemiah knew that his heart was aligned with their Supreme Ruler's, and that was all the security he needed. "Shouldn't you walk in the fear of our God?" he barked, ordering them to return everything to the people (Nehemiah 5:9). Stunned, the nobles could say nothing in reply but "we will not demand anything more from them [the poor]. We will do as you say" (Nehemiah 5:11–12).

This is just one example of Nehemiah's great heart for his people, and he will be remembered for it (Nehemiah 5:19).

There are five practical elements that help us express our love and care for those we serve on a daily basis by strengthening our relationships with them. These are important because it doesn't matter how smart you are, how gifted you might be, or how much you know about vision and strategy. If you don't know how to connect and get along with people, you won't make it far as a leader. Conversely, the better your relationships, the fewer conflicts you experience, and the greater your confidence becomes.

Five Practical Principles to Strengthen Your Relationships

1. Value Simplicity and Intimacy

Relationships are personal. Even though we live in an age when connecting with others online is the norm, real relationships can't be deeply developed or lived out from a distance for long.

One of the most striking stories of personal connection in the New Testament is the post-resurrection account of Jesus having breakfast with seven of the disciples on the beach (John 21:1–14). He didn't need to do that to accomplish his mission, but he chose to. Relationships involve intentional choices and an effort to be close.

The seven disciples had fished all night and caught nothing. Jesus called out to them, "Friends, haven't you any fish?" (John 21:5). They said no, and Jesus told them to throw the net on the other side. They caught so many they couldn't haul the net in.

Jesus called them his friends, made them breakfast, and sat on the beach talking with them. A lake, sand, charcoal, some fish and bread, and heart. It was simple and intimate. Don't overcomplicate or overthink relationships. Invest time, stay close, and open your heart.

2. Listening from the Heart Immediately Deepens a Relationship

Smartphones, time compression (others' expectation of how you spend your time), and busy schedules (your own expectation of how you spend your time) have resulted in losing the fine art of listening. Most of us are in a rush and want the "headlines only" version. When I'm the one talking, I find myself overly concerned about making most of everything I say brief for fear of taking too much time. It's not a healthy practice.

In fact, when I'm with someone and give them my full and undivided attention and truly listen, they often say something like, "I can't remember the last time someone wanted to hear what I had to say and actually listened to me. Thank you."

Listening is a gift that connects you at a heart level. Turn your phone off, look the person in the eyes, and listen. It's amazing what happens.

3. Admit When You're Wrong and Say I'm Sorry   *Forgive me!*

It's a common and equally unfortunate trait among leaders to fear being wrong. We all mess up on occasion. When we do, we need to apologize. Say I'm sorry if you have hurt or offended someone. Your genuine humility will go a long way to strengthening your relationships. We all make mistakes, and sometimes we don't know what to do and need help. Owning those times gains you credibility and builds trust.

Refrain from unnecessarily defending yourself. The art of debate rarely helps build closeness. And while I'm not suggesting you let someone take advantage of you, "winning and losing" is never a good approach to cultivating meaningful relationships. Extend grace whenever you can.

4. Add Value to Others

As I mentioned in the story of Jesus and breakfast on the beach, he showed the disciples how to catch fish in their moment of need. Jesus helped them turn failure into success and get their work done. He added value to their practical lives, and he engaged them in a way that would develop their faith. Again, he added more value.

Poor leaders receive more than they give. Average leaders choose the fastest way to tend to a relationship, which always feels more transactional than transformational. Great leaders choose their relationships wisely, invest deeply, and always add value.

Again, don't make relationships complicated. They tend to do that on their own. Keep it simple. Adding value might look like sending a book you know would be helpful and meaningful to someone you lead, giving someone an idea that will help them move forward in their business or personal life, introducing them to another leader they could not meet on their own, or something as simple as writing a note or praying for them. Always add value!

5. Laughter Is the Best Medicine

Life is often serious and filled with daily pressures. The people you lead face financial worries, health concerns, and family conflicts. As we lead, comfort, and guide them, we take these matters seriously as well.

However, take every opportunity you can to bring joy and laughter to those you lead, love, and serve. It's truly life giving. Hospital visits and camping are similar to me. I love nature, I just don't want to get any of it on me. Whether the bugs are those creepy crawlers in your sleeping bag or a virus in your system, neither one puts me in my happy place. But I make hospital visits anyway because they are important and valuable to those I serve. When I do, I always look for a moment to help the person smile or laugh. Being lighthearted in a serious world is always a good idea. Whether in a board meeting, a one-on-one conversation, or as part of your teaching style, lighten up at the right moments. You'll be glad you did, and so will those around you.

> Take every opportunity you can to bring joy and laughter to those you lead, love, and serve.

With a heart set to care about people, you are poised to communicate an optimistic message, the topic of our next chapter.

CHAPTER 14

COMMUNICATION

LIVE AND CONVEY AN OPTIMISTIC MESSAGE

Optimism is the faith that leads to achievement.
Nothing can be done without hope and confidence.
—Helen Keller

My friend James is the senior pastor of a multisite church with an attendance of nearly three thousand. He is a very positive, high-energy, and upbeat guy, but one time when he called, I could tell something was up.

One of his campus pastors had decided to leave and start a church about two miles from their existing main campus. This campus pastor was openly inviting people he was connected with in the church to join him, saying negative things about James, causing intentional division.

He didn't have to say much more for a question to surface. How, in a situation like this, can a leader overcome so much discouragement and still communicate an optimistic message? Let's be realistic, it isn't exactly the moment to stand up and say, "Hey, let's all go to Disneyland!"

James and the board were forced to consult legal counsel, make tough decisions, and develop a message that was transparent and truthful, yet somehow still optimistic. Even though the board members were all godly leaders, they struggled with what to do. James's confidence was shaken as well. Further, the campus pastor was a younger staff member James had personally developed and invested in heavily. This felt like a deep betrayal.

The day came when James had to address the leaders of the church, and he chose the high road. He began with honesty, about his hurt and disappointment, but then moved into an authentic and hope-filled vision for the future, inspiring others to love and show faith, in spite of what this difficult experience would cost the church. He worked hard to never speak poorly of the campus pastor to them. Incredibly, he even closed by praying for the successful launch of the new church and the ministry of the departing pastor.

Of course, the story is so much more involved than we have space for here, but you get the picture. This leads me to my original question: How could James be so optimistic in the middle of such a difficult and hurtful situation? It's because of who he is and the choices he makes.

James was definitely hurt, and for a while even angry, but he understood that despite the personal attack, loss, and adversity, having a negative disposition or retaliating wouldn't help anything. He is a fantastic leader who intentionally chooses to find the good, make the best of it, and then communicate an optimistic message. The choices he makes, along with his internal bent toward a positive spirit, gives a tremendous boost to his confidence and the confidence of those around him.

Like James, good leaders communicate confidence by the words they speak and the tone in which they are spoken. An optimistic message can only come from an optimistic life and a positive spirit. Therefore it is an integral part of your daily life, and it has a profound effect on your level of influence. In essence, effective leaders communicate a message of hope. This is an essential daily discipline of a confident leader.

> An optimistic message can only come from an optimistic life and a positive spirit.

I'm not suggesting that as a leader you never have a bad day, get discouraged, or second-guess yourself. But your confidence will surely wear thin and your influence may decline without a positive attitude toward life in general. A hope-filled disposition can boost your leadership confidence like few other things.

My friend Ashley Wooldridge, the senior pastor at Christ's Church of the Valley in Phoenix, Arizona, is a living example of this.

Interview with Ashley Wooldridge

Born in Wilcox, Arizona, a small town of just one thousand people, Ashley grew up with the blessing of knowing his neighbors and having a strong sense of community. The church where his dad served as an elder and his mom played the piano was, of course, small too.

Ashley said, "We all knew everyone, which kept me real, because you can't hide. On my dad's teacher's salary and with three other siblings, we didn't grow up with much, but we had everything that mattered. That shaped my values about possessions and relationships. It taught me what money could and could not buy."[1]

By the time he finished high school, Ashley had not yet received his calling into ministry, but nevertheless chose to attend a Christian college, majoring in both business and the Bible. Right after graduating, he married his wife, Jaime, and then launched a corporate career at Intel, where he stayed for the next eight years. It was then that God finally gave him clarity about his call.

Ashley said, "God made it clear that I was to spend the rest of my life serving the local church. I told God I'd do anything. I didn't know what it would be, but my vision was 'the local church should be the most well-led organization in the world.'"[2]

Regarding things he learned during his Intel years, Ashley said, "When you are trying to bring solutions through change, you have to rely on influence, and influence depends on communication. If the message isn't positive and filled with hope, people aren't interested."[3]

Ashley eventually joined the staff at Christ's Church of the Valley as an executive pastor. In less than a decade, he was teaching on a regular basis and then was entrusted with overseeing the executive team. In 2017, he was invited to become the next senior pastor for Christ's Church, whose weekly attendance is thirty-five thousand with ten campuses and four hundred on staff.

Ashley is a gifted and highly relational leader. He has a strong, strategic mind and is an excellent communicator. One of Ashley's clearest qualities is his consistent optimistic outlook.

On the importance of continually communicating a positive message,

Ashley said, "If you don't connect, it's difficult to get anyone to buy into what you're saying. Whether it's a one-on-one meeting or teaching to thousands, people connect with a positive spirit and they are drawn to joy.

"A simple smile does something," he continued. "A smile is very spiritual because it communicates something that comes from deep inside—from the Holy Spirit. I've not always been the smartest person in the room, but people could hear me because they sense my joy and know it's real. You can have the best idea, but if you can't communicate it in a way that people can hear, it doesn't matter."[4]

> "A smile is very spiritual because it communicates something that comes from deep inside—from the Holy Spirit."
> —ASHLEY WOOLDRIDGE

This begs a question: How can a leader sustain a disposition of hope and communicate an authentically optimistic attitude in the face of conflict and problems?

In a reflective moment during our conversation, Ashley said, "We have to maintain a deep realization that we'll never have a day without a problem. However, God is always in position to provide solutions to the problems we're facing. Further, we don't have to face those problems alone.

"Problems cause leaders to become discouraged. When I face difficult situations and get discouraged, I quickly recall God's track record in my life. His batting average is a thousand. He's never let me down. Not once. That doesn't mean everything goes my way, but he's always been with me.

"We all deal with problems that discourage us. Some leaders can pull themselves up from the basement faster than others because of how they view their problems. They're just part of life, and we solve them one at time. That translates to greater confidence and a naturally optimistic style of communication."[5]

Wrapping up our conversation, I asked Ashley about his confidence as a leader. He answered, "My confidence comes from a deep sense of being truly dependent on God in every situation. I'm not qualified on my own. I did not ask for my role and never once asked to preach. But God qualifies me. Time after time I've been invited to the table, to new opportunities, because someone has seen something in me. That inspires confidence in me. I've learned that it's God. He sees something in me, and Ephesians 3:20

kicks into gear: 'Now to him who is able to do immeasurably more than all we ask or imagine, according to his power that is at work within us.'"[6]

What can we learn from my interview with Ashley? It's clear to me that problem solving, tough decisions, and leading change are all part of your daily discipline as a leader. Your ability to sustain a positive spirit and optimistic viewpoint is essential, not only for your confidence but for the confidence of those you lead.

It has often been said, "Your problem is not your problem. It's all about what you do with your problem." That's true. It's how you see it, respond to it, and take appropriate action.

For example, your church may be growing slowly or perhaps not at all. And as a leader that's your responsibility, or at least in part, depending on your role. Your perspective will strongly influence the outcome. Some leaders will sink into despair and get stuck, and some will energize others to rise to the challenge and take action. Words they communicate will always match their disposition. For you to communicate an optimistic message, you first must believe that message yourself.

There are several responses to the daily challenges of leadership that will break down your ability to communicate in a way that encourages people to live for Christ and inspire them toward the vision of your church. Let's take a brief look at five.

Five Responses That Break Down Your Optimism

1. Doubt

On my best days I still doubt a little. I think all leaders who are honest with themselves do. The reason is because we can't predict the future. We can never be fully certain about the outcomes of our leadership while making progress and taking new territory. However, you need not allow doubt to swallow up your vision and dreams.

> You may not be certain, but you can still be confident.

You may not be certain, but you can still be confident. Why? Like Ashley said, God's batting average is a thousand. He is with you, and it is his church. Remember your calling, remember what God has done, and focus on your vision.

2. Worry

Worry is common among leaders. I'm not referring to the hand-wringing kind of chronic worry that may lead to anxiety, but to overthinking or being overly concerned about something that, most of the time, never happens or you can't change.

Remember, if you can't change it, it's not a problem; it's a fact of life. We solve problems and adapt to facts of life. For example, if your income falls below budget, that's a problem you can take action on. If the community your church is located in is changing, you adapt. For the short list of real problems remaining, take action.

The bottom line is that worry isn't helpful or productive, and it rarely if ever changes anything. It definitely drains your energy and robs you of your ability to authentically talk with others from a heart of optimism.

3. Cynicism

It's rare that anyone begins ministry as a cynic. But in time, after enough people have let you down, disappointed, or hurt you, believing the best in people can become difficult. In fact, it can lead to difficulty in trusting and relying on people and even beginning to believe the worst in them.

For example, if enough volunteers have let you down, you may find it difficult to recruit, train, and empower more volunteers. This has a significant effect on how you think and communicate with others. Breaking the cycle of cynicism begins with beginning to trust again and starting to intentionally look for the best in people. You will find what you look for.

4. Negativity

A young pastor once said about himself, "I'm not a pessimist, I'm a realist." That may have been true, but what I explained to him in a candid coaching moment was that people often receive him as negative. His words and their tone were not perceived as full of faith and optimistic. I knew he had a positive nature in him, but it needed to be coached out. He needed to learn to express it better.

I'm not advocating the Pollyanna syndrome (an excessively or blindly optimistic point of view). Nor do I believe in the Chicken Little syndrome (believing the sky is falling and the world is coming to an end). It may take some coaching to do this well, but you can be honest about life and yet still be positive. Our hope in Christ and faith in eternal life is our platform, and foundation for a positive perspective.

5. Fatigue

Overwork, too much stress, and too little sleep are major components that contribute to the breakdown of your ability to communicate in a positive manner. Fatigue causes you to lose perspective, and when combined with the weight of your leadership responsibility, it often results in an edge to your communication that pushes people away, rather than drawing them toward you.

> **Fatigue causes you to lose perspective.**

The good news is that fatigue may be the easiest to remedy from this list. Get some rest! Seriously, resist the temptation to work on your day off, and make a real effort to get a good night's sleep every night.

Five Choices That Build Up Your Optimism

1. Don't Let Your Critics Get Under Your Skin

Leaders attract critics. If for no other reason than because leaders create change, and in general, people don't like change. It's also true that the larger group you lead, the more critics you will gather. Therefore, learning to handle your critics is an important skill.

One year, 12Stone Church did not hold church services when Christmas fell on a Sunday. We chose to honor our thousands of volunteers by freeing up that special time so they could be with their families. Instead, we held Christmas Eve services to celebrate the birth of Christ. Our congregation loved the beautiful service, but the critics, the vast majority of whom were not part of 12Stone, let us have it for "canceling church on Christmas!" We did our best to receive the criticism graciously and respond with kindness, but we chose to focus on the positive nature of the wonderful Christmas Eve services and our amazing volunteers getting some well-deserved time with their families.

When dealing with a critic on a more personal level, it's important to listen and learn, but don't allow the specific criticism or the person delivering it get to you. Avoid becoming defensive, listen for truth, own what you need to own, and translate what you have learned to growth-oriented action. Taking that intentional and positive approach not only supports your level of optimism, but your poise, discipline, and self-control strengthen your confidence.

2. Keep Your Heart Set on the Vision

Your vision is central to communication on both a personal and church-wide level. God has given you that vision, and it carries great weight. It's inspiring and life giving. It brings strength and potential for momentum. However, it's easy to get lost in the day-to-day details and challenges of ministry and lose sight of the big picture. When that happens, the words you speak can become derailed and lose their optimistic flavor. You are at risk of your conversations missing the positive passion they once had.

Take a few minutes each day, perhaps as part of your prayer time, to reset your heart and passion for the vision of your church. There is always hope in the preferred future you have made clear to your congregation. Your confidence will be recharged, and your faith will be lifted. As a result, your communication will once again be positive.

3. Invest Time with Positive and Like-Minded People

As a pastor, part of my responsibility is to shepherd people, and it's my privilege to love and care for them. Not often, but on occasion, this will connect me with someone who could find something wrong with ice cream, puppies, and the streets of gold in heaven. They have a unique gift of cornering their prey like a velociraptor hunting for dinner. Okay, maybe it's not *that* bad, but you get the picture.

> Can you name three to five people who fill you up with whom you connect on a regular basis?

There are people whom you love and

care for that drain you of your energy. That's okay. But you need significant time with people who fill you back up. You need time with leaders and friends who invest in you, care about you, and help you become a better leader. Choose these insiders wisely. Can you name three to five people who fill you up with whom you connect on a regular basis?

These close and invaluable people in your life must be positive in nature and have an optimistic view of the future. They are the special people who add value to you and boost your confidence, just as you do for them and others. They are like-minded because they share the same values, passion for the church, and love for people as you do.

4. Fill Your Mind and Heart with Uplifting Content

I'll admit I'm part of the social media world, and there is much about it that is good. But I can also tell you it can consume your time if you're not discerning and careful. It can feed you content that is not helpful or positive in nature. That's true with nearly any form of media.

You have a limited amount of time to fill your mind and heart with meaningful content. Make the best of it. We all love a good movie and other forms of entertainment. But for the bulk of your input, what are you choosing?

Read, listen, and study widely, but always start with Scripture as your foundation. Discover your favorite authors, podcasts, teachers, and thought leaders. This is a basic daily discipline for effective leadership and increased confidence.

When do you set aside time to fill your mind and heart? If you do this every day, or at least five days a week, you'll be surprised at how much you can gain in about fifty minutes a day. Remember, it's not the amount of content but what you do with it. What are you learning and how are you applying it?

5. Choose Joy

The apostle Paul is a radical example of choosing joy.

Five times I received from the Jews the forty lashes minus one. Three times I was beaten with rods, once I was pelted with stones, three times

I was shipwrecked, I spent a night and a day in the open sea, I have been constantly on the move. I have been in danger from rivers, in danger from bandits, in danger from my fellow Jews, in danger from Gentiles; in danger in the city, in danger in the country, in danger at sea; and in danger from false believers. I have labored and toiled and have often gone without sleep; I have known hunger and thirst and have often gone without food; I have been cold and naked. (2 Corinthians 11:24–27)

This is the same guy who sang while in prison (Acts 16:25) and endured great suffering for the sake of the gospel (2 Corinthians 11:23–29). Meanwhile, if they run out of chocolate chip cookies at my favorite restaurant, I'm tempted to write my congressman.

> **Choosing joy is an intentional decision for all of us as leaders.**

Choosing joy is an intentional decision for all of us as leaders. Joy is contagious, first in our own souls, then to others. It will lift your confidence and help you communicate with an optimistic flavor.

Nehemiah understood this principle of positive communication. As we move to the next narrative of Nehemiah's leadership, notice how he handled a complicated situation.

NEHEMIAH'S POSITIVE COMMUNICATION

"Then Nehemiah the governor, Ezra . . . and the Levites who were instructing the people said to them all, 'This day is holy to the LORD your God. Do not mourn or weep.' For all the people had been weeping as they listened to the words of the Law. Nehemiah said, '. . . Do not grieve, for the joy of the LORD is your strength'" (Nehemiah 8:9–10).

The wall was finished, so now what? The grand project of rebuilding Jerusalem had temporarily unified everyone behind a common cause, but now that it was done, what would hold them together? A city is really made up of its people, not its walls or buildings.

To truly build Jerusalem, it required building its community, which required a common culture. Without a shared culture, no team or group of people can bond with one another. Nehemiah instinctively understood this, so he set about organizing everyone (Nehemiah 7:1–3). Next, God inspired him to call together a grand assembly in the city (Nehemiah 7:5).

For the Jewish people, there is only one logical common culture that could be adopted: a culture centered around the Torah. So Ezra the priest began to read publicly from God's Law. Hearing the sacred words and realizing just how far they'd missed the mark of God's will for them, the people began to weep and mourn.

Yet Nehemiah understood that the public assembly could only be successful if the people walked away positively inspired to pursue God's will together on an ongoing basis. Slinking away into the sunset as defeated sinners before they'd even begun would be a tragic loss after so much success.

Accordingly, Nehemiah stood before them and said, "Do not mourn or weep . . . Go and enjoy choice food and sweet drinks, and send some to those who have nothing prepared. This day is holy to our Lord. Do not grieve, for the joy of the Lord is your strength" (Nehemiah 8:9–10).

Then he and the leaders under him continued to encourage the people to respond with rejoicing, and thus, he successfully turned the day around. "Then all the people went away to eat and drink, to send portions of food and to celebrate with great joy, because they now understood the words that had been made known to them" (Nehemiah 8:12).

Positive communication from leadership inspires a positive response from the people, and this in turn creates more confidence in the leader.

As we head to the last chapter, reflect on the primary concepts of the first fourteen chapters and how they will help you develop other leaders as you develop yourself.

CHAPTER 15

MENTORING

DEVELOP OTHER LEADERS INTENTIONALLY

The growth and development of people is
the highest calling of leadership.
—HARVEY FIRESTONE

After twelve years of serving as a law enforcement officer with a metro-Atlanta police department, Steve Finn and his wife, Dawn, sensed God stirring them to open a children's home. For a year they prayed for God to confirm this call by moving others to speak into their lives but without telling anyone what they were feeling. Steve also began asking God to provide the preparation he needed.

In 2004, God prompted me to invite Steve to be part of Joshua's Men, a one-year intensive leadership development program, along with six other men.[1] God used it to make Steve's vision clear.

It was this community of men sharpening each other, developing each other as leaders, and speaking into Steve's life that challenged him to go after the vision God had placed in his heart. Steve would tell you today that without it he would not have had the confidence to move forward.

Steve's leadership legacy began in 2005 with the birth of a vision for Chestnut Mountain Ranch, launched in Morgantown, West Virginia. Steve and Dawn had sensed God's calling was very specific to that state, probably because of its serious economic struggles and the fact that West Virginia consistently ranks among the highest in the country for children living in poverty. A few of his friends from the leadership development group helped Steve write a business plan and conduct a needs assessment for West Virginia and the Appalachian culture.

Once that was finished, it was time to take action.

Steve and Dawn and their three kids packed their belongings and moved to Morgantown. The going was quite tough at first. There was even one day their checking account dropped down to a stress-inducing $25.54.

Yet God did provide. The vision was clear, and the work slowly began to get off the ground. Today, Chestnut Mountain Ranch is a thriving Christ-centered home, nationally accredited school, and community that equips boys to overcome their past and prepares them for their future.

Their debt-free model is flourishing with two residence houses now complete, a third one under construction, and at least five more envisioned for the future. In 2020, they are projected to receive more than one hundred requests from parents of children who need the hope and guidance their program provides.

> Leadership development is in some ways like prayer. It's hard to do it wrong, but you do need to start.

Steve and Dawn's leadership legacy is growing strong. Sixty boys have already completed the program, with a vision for hundreds more to come. Steve took what was poured into him from his Joshua's Men group and now invests it in others. He, Dawn, and their staff develop young men to become good husbands, fathers, and leaders. Generations to come will be changed for the good.

This is a great picture of *your* potential legacy through mentoring others to become leaders. The details of your story will be different, but your vision is just as important. You might begin by developing a small group of leaders on your staff, volunteer leaders in the congregation, or maybe even just one leader in your church.

Leadership development is in some ways like prayer. It's hard to do it wrong, but you do need to start. That said, you can also get better at it with practice and learning from those who have gone before you. For example, you can learn from an incredible developer of leaders like Jerry Hurley.

A Conversation with Jerry Hurley

It's common knowledge that God loves to raise up the humblest people to do great things, as it brings him more glory. In the case of Jerry Hurley, God chose an "unlikely person to lead" (as Jerry describes himself), and he raised him up to be the team development leader of the largest church in the United States.

Born in El Paso, Texas, a veritable melting pot of American and Hispanic cultures, to a hardworking middle-class family, there was nothing immediately obvious to the outside world to indicate the level of leadership Jerry would one day achieve. His father was an engineer with the Southern Pacific Railroad, and his mother worked for the government.

He ended up marrying "the girl next door." Jerry first met his future wife, Annette, at just ten years of age at a summer band camp and he walked her home from practice one day. At sixteen they began to date, and they got married immediately after high school.

Jerry became a Christian at a young age but didn't sense a call to ministry until he was almost thirty. Yet he didn't know what to do with that call, where to go or how to start to answer it, so he spoke with a deacon in the small Baptist church where he was attending. The deacon responded, "If you are sure you're called, then trust God will open a door. When he does, go through it. From now until then, prepare."[2] That's exactly what Jerry did. He started by serving in that small Baptist church in Texas.

While discovering exactly what God had in store for him, he continued in his corporate career. He ended up working for Target, where he eventually became a district team leader responsible for eleven stores and twenty-six hundred employees. I can still hear the wonder in Jerry's voice when he said, "I had no idea that my experience in a fortune 100 company would lay the groundwork for what God would have me do years later."[3]

Now, leading as part of the executive team at Life Church based in Edmond, Oklahoma, Jerry is the team development leader with staff leadership responsibilities for 650 employees, covering 33 campus locations in 10 states, and currently averaging 92,000 people a weekend. This is quite a difference from when he first joined the staff in 1998. Back then, there was only one location and six hundred people. Jerry is not just one of the most gifted leaders I know and a great thinker, he is also a man with a humble and generous heart.

I asked Jerry what motivated his passion to mentor leaders, and what has kept him going as a developer of people through the years. His heartfelt response was simply, "I've always been able to see potential in people, and I love helping people grow."[4]

The connection between development and confidence was obvious. As staff become better leaders, their confidence rises. And the same is true for the developers of leaders.

When it comes to mentoring and leadership development, Jerry and the team have developed the following four core pillars on which they've built their developmental culture. It's pure genius.

1. People develop best in their challenging role.
2. All growth is born out of self-awareness.
3. It is difficult for growth to occur without trusted relationships.
4. People grow best when they own their own growth.

I asked Jerry to describe his confidence as a leader, and he said, "I'm an INFP, not an ENTJ. Artists and writers are more likely INFPs, but it's not the common leadership profile. I'm an unlikely person to lead."[5]

Jerry continued, "It's all been a supernatural thing. God's been in it the whole time. I have a much bigger sense of inadequacy than confidence. I've always felt as though I'm not living up to my potential.

"There was time lasting about six to nine months at Life Church when I was serving both as an executive pastor and a campus pastor, working hard, but felt the church had grown past me, at least the way I was trying to do it. I thought I was in the way, so I needed to step away.

"When these thoughts are in your head, it doesn't take long for them to get reinforced and take root. I considered resigning. Then God led me to a passage in the life of David. The essence of the message was God telling David he was the one who took him as a shepherd and made him king (2 Samuel 7:8). Obviously, I'm not a king, but I knew what God meant. That changed *everything*.

> All growth is born out of self-awareness.

"My thinking changed to 'God, you put me in this role and you will remove me when it's time. Put it in Craig's[6] heart if it's time for me to go. Otherwise I will stay and lead until you let me know my time is done.' That stopped those thoughts.

"God could have chosen anyone else, but he chose me. My best is enough. My confidence is secure in that thought. I connect with the line in the movie *Chariots of Fire* when Eric Liddell says, 'I believe God made me for a purpose, but he also made me fast. And when I run, I feel his pleasure.'"[7]

Jerry finished by saying, "This is who I'm supposed to be and what I'm to do, and I sense God's pleasure."[8]

We Are All Responsible to Develop Leaders

Jerry, of course, is not the only one who is called to develop leaders. If you want to reach the fullest potential of your vision, you will need other growing leaders to help you achieve it. And there is nothing that supercharges your personal growth as a leader quite like developing other leaders. This

> There is nothing that supercharges your personal growth as a leader quite like developing other leaders.

naturally builds your confidence because you served as the catalyst for the growth you see in others. The consistent discipline of developing leaders is vital to your overall success as a leader.

My book *Amplified Leadership* is dedicated in its entirety to the subject of developing leaders. It will serve as a great companion to this chapter.

Jesus Modeled the Way for Us

As I study the Bible from Moses and Joshua to Paul and Timothy, there is a pattern of developing and raising up leaders. Jesus himself developed leaders. He chose twelve through whom he would unleash his kingdom on earth. Jesus didn't *need* the twelve disciples; he could have lived, died, resurrected, and chosen another way. He didn't have to bother with that small group arguing over who was the greatest and who lacked faith, whining about their status, and asking a lot of frustrating questions. But working through other leaders was God's plan from the beginning. Jesus modeled development for us. His pattern was to spend time with them, care for them, teach them, correct them, empower them, and send them. That's a great picture of leadership development.

Five Proven Principles and Practices to Develop Leaders

1. Deepen the Relationship

As a mentor, developing leaders always begins by first establishing a strong relationship and investing in a way that deepens that relationship. It doesn't matter if you've known the person or group of people for some time or if you've recently met. A heart-to-heart connection is essential to establish the trust needed for their greatest growth. That connection is built on a foundation of authenticity, which always includes open and honest conversation. The best approach to these coaching conversations is a balanced combination of straightforward truth and uplifting encouragement.

Clarifying expectations is another vital element for a productive and deepening relationship. It became obvious that one young leader I was mentoring was disappointed in the process. I asked what was bothering him. He said he thought we'd be hanging out and having dinner together, sometimes with our wives. It's almost always about something expected that didn't happen as anticipated.

> Authentic connection and clear expectations help build trust.

Don't hesitate to make sure the expectations are agreed upon. I'm not suggesting that you make it feel formal or like a contract. Keep it warm and relational, but make sure it's clear. Discuss elements like time investment, who sets the agenda, progress goals, accountability, and so on.

Authentic connection and clear expectations help build trust, which is the foundation for any effective approach to developing leaders. This mutual trust requires two things: that they know you have their best interest at heart, and that you know they are fully committed and all in. This produces a mutual connection and bond of trust that is strong and engaging. Here's a good test: Do you look forward to your next time together?

2. Get on Their Agenda

One of the mistakes I've made in developing leaders is answering questions they aren't asking. I take off on a subject I think is important and they should hear, but it's not really of interest to them at the moment. It comes from my passion and enthusiasm to be helpful. I want the best for them. But I've learned to get on their agenda, and that starts with my asking questions and listening carefully to their answers. You may need to redirect the focus on occasion, especially for young or inexperienced leaders, but it always starts with where they are, not what's on your mind.

Specific questions tailored to them are best, but here's a list of ten general questions you can start with that will help you establish a deeper relationship. Please note that they are not in any order and some are one-time questions, and some can be asked regularly. And remember, just because you are in a supervisory relationship at a church or business, don't assume you already know the answers. Give others the opportunity to share authentically and receive their answers with openness and enthusiasm.

- Where are you headed in the next few years, and are you making progress?
- What do you want to get better at and why?
- Are you happy with your job?
- What's the biggest problem you're trying to solve right now?
- What's holding you back from becoming the person and leader you want to become?
- What was it like growing up in your home?
- What specific skill do you most need to develop now?
- How would you rate your leadership confidence on a scale of 1 to 10? Why do you rate yourself that way?
- How are things at home?
- What do you expect from this relationship?

These questions will help you discover who they are, what they want, and how best to help them grow. On a practical level, each time you meet, have the person you're developing bring the agenda and his or her questions they want to work on together with you.

3. Concentrate on Their Strengths

It's always best to focus on a leader's strengths, but there are times when you must invest time in his or her struggles. Use this simple but effective picture for assessment to determine their "zone":

- Strength zone = They are swimming well, making progress.
- Struggle zone = They are treading water, just maintaining.
- Stuck zone = They are going under, in danger of drowning.

I was coaching a young executive pastor who is a strong leader, smart, and gifted in strategy. We were appropriately focused on his strength zone and leveraging his strategic abilities, but things kept blowing up on him. It didn't take long to discover that, while he was capable of developing good relationships, he was not giving them the time they needed. I slowed things down and turned to his struggle zone. His first step was to ask forgiveness and restore key relationships. He knew the importance of relationships and cared about people, so we also invested some time in what was going on within him that caused him to ignore the relationships. Then we got back to his strength zone as soon as possible. Here's a four-point guideline for you to use:

- Pay attention to both strengths and struggles but focus on strengths.
- Keep a fluid and simple plan based on one to three items at a time.
- If they're in the stuck zone, set aside skill for the moment and focus on soul. (We'll address this in point five below.)
- Have the tough conversations and be generous with encouragement.

Remember, if you are developing a small group of leaders, which is often ideal, they all need some one-on-one time.

4. Emphasize Practice and Progress

Leadership development is never merely a transfer of information. The purpose is providing application opportunities that result in measurable growth. And growth requires practice. This means working on a specific skill that they can't do until they can. For example, anyone can cut vegetables, but only highly skilled home cooks and chefs can cut quickly and accurately, which means cutting them all the same size so they cook at the same rate and are therefore consistent. It's like the perfect french fry; if they are not cut to the same size, they don't cook the same, and you will get some burned or soggy fries.

The same idea is true in leadership. As a mentor, you help leaders you are developing discover the skill gaps that prevent them from reaching their goals and coach them to a place where they can eventually do what they once could not. A good mentor brings out the best in those they develop!

A pastor I was mentoring was having trouble truly learning the skill of empowering others. He understood the components of empowering, such as giving responsibility, training, authority, and so forth, but when it came right down to it, he simply couldn't let go. He wanted to, but something within him needed to hold on to control. Yet he accepted my challenge to bite the bullet and practice empowerment. He took on bite-size pieces of the problem by first letting his worship leader pick out the songs without his input, and then letting his small group director select the curriculum without running it by him first. It was challenging for him to let go of those things, but the breakthrough was worth it.

> Leadership development is never merely a transfer of information.

You might be developing someone in recruiting, communication, how to connect with others, or in listening skills. The possibilities are nearly endless. Whatever it may be, always watch for progress as you coach and mentor. Effort and dedication are required, and improvement is essential. In what way is the leader you are developing better today than he or she was six months ago?

5. Listen for the Holy Spirit's Guidance

The beauty and power of developing others as Christian leaders is that you and I do not need to rely on our own human talent. God has given you experience and insight, and where you lack wisdom, you can ask for it. "If any of you lacks wisdom, you should ask God, who gives generously to all without finding fault, and it will be given to you. But when you ask, you must believe and not doubt, because the one who doubts is like a wave of the sea, blown and tossed by the wind" (James 1:5–6).

> **We are challenged to believe and not doubt.**

God is generous with wisdom, but you can see another element of your confidence in play here. We are challenged to believe and not doubt. You can see in verse 6 that leaders are often plagued with second-guessing. The more you practice listening for and discerning the voice of the Holy Spirit, the greater your confidence becomes.

Ask the Holy Spirit to give you insight in the following three areas as you develop leaders:

- *Their specific need for soul contentment.* How naturally and authentically do they demonstrate inner peace, personal poise, and overall gratitude?
- *Their specific need for skill improvement.* What competency improvements are needed for them to become better leaders?
- *Their specific need for spiritual maturity.* Do they love God and others and serve people well, especially with their families? Do they listen for, hear, and obey God's voice?

Nehemiah understood the need to develop other leaders and demonstrated godly wisdom in the process.

NEHEMIAH'S WISDOM

When Nehemiah arrived in Jerusalem the second time, he was greatly dismayed. After finishing the wall and instituting many reforms, he had returned to King Artaxerxes in Persia to report their progress and reaffirm loyalty. Before leaving, though, he raised up other leaders to ensure progress was not lost in his absence.

A wise leader knows there is a hard limit to their potential influence without others carrying out the vision. To amplify his leadership, Nehemiah knew he needed to raise up leaders under him and train them to lead others: "I put in charge of Jerusalem my brother Hanani, along with Hananiah the commander of the citadel, because he was a man of integrity and feared God more than most people do" (Nehemiah 7:1–2).

Nehemiah also recognized he needed to mentor men of integrity, not just ones who were skilled or "connected." He trained them with specifics about how to proceed while he was gone, including how to lead others (Nehemiah 7:3).

Unfortunately, while Nehemiah was out of the country, Tobiah, the enemy ruler who had previously sought to undermine him at every turn, successfully made inroads into corrupting Jerusalem. However, he was only able to do it in the one weak spot Nehemiah had not shored up. Nehemiah had placed leaders in charge of the civil government and Jerusalem's security, but there had remained an area outside his influence: the temple. "I learned about the evil thing Eliashib [the priest] had done in providing Tobiah a room in the courts of the house of God" (Nehemiah 13:7).

Tobiah was using God's house as storage for his household goods, and the things of God had been moved elsewhere. The Levites and the musicians had been sent home, so worship and instruction had ceased. Also, because of Tobiah and the corrupted Eliashib's influence, tithes were down, the Sabbath was being ignored, and Jerusalemites were beginning to marry foreign women again, which was allowing idol worship to creep back in.

Nehemiah took action once more. He challenged the officials, asking, "Why is the house of God neglected?" He cast Tobiah's things into the street, threatened to arrest the merchants defiling the Sabbath, and acted radically to restore the house of God (Nehemiah 13:8–28). Yet it wasn't enough, so he didn't stop there. It was time to mentor more leaders.

"I put Shelemiah the priest, Zadok the scribe, and a Levite named Pedaiah in charge of the storerooms and made Hanan . . . their assistant, because they were considered trustworthy. They were made responsible for distributing the supplies to their fellow Levites . . . I [also] purified the priests and the Levites of everything foreign, and assigned them duties, each to his own task" (Nehemiah 13:13, 30).

In the end, Nehemiah's reforms would be the basis of a restored Judaism that would prepare the way for Jesus. But he didn't do it alone. He mentored and empowered leaders to help him accomplish the task.

You have finished reading this book, but this is just the beginning. Confidence isn't an overnight process, it's a great journey, and you have what it takes. The process is about unlocking your confidence and putting it into practice. God designed it in you to match the divine assignments he brings your way.

My prayer is that God will provide a clear abundance of his presence and power so that, when combined with your prayers and effort, you will develop the consistent and authentic, life-giving confidence that will help you become the leader you were always meant to be.

May these words from the Lord to Joshua serve as a specific prayer over you: "Be strong and very courageous. Be careful to obey all the law my servant Moses gave you; do not turn from it to the right or to the left, that you may be successful wherever you go" (Joshua 1:7).

ACKNOWLEDGMENTS

The vision, writing, and completion of this book would not have happened without the significant contributions of others. I'm blessed to have such friends and colleagues along with the never-ending support of Patti, my beautiful wife of thirty-nine years.

My heartfelt gratitude and appreciation are difficult to put into words, but I must at least name each person so you know how this project found its way into your hands.

Thank you:

Charlie Wetzel, for the initial encouragement, brainstorming, and creative input to help move this project from concept to reality. Without your invaluable help I might have just written a book on why chocolate chip cookies are considered the eighth wonder of the world.

Bryan Mason, for the biblical research and writing of the Old Testament narratives on Moses, David, and Nehemiah, and our many conversations as we worked through the drafts. Thanks, too, for the awesome white tea from Boulder Creek Coffee in Lawrenceville, Georgia.

Carolyn Reed Master, for the gifted wordsmithing that made my writing better and the research that helped me keep high standards of writing integrity. You are a true gift and delight to work with, and I love that you strive for world-class quality.

Kadi Cole, Sam Chand, Jo Anne Lyon, David Drury, Carey Nieuwhof, John Maxwell, Jenni Catron, Chris Hodges, Crawford Loritts, Ashley Wooldridge, and Jerry Hurley, for your generous gift of time and transparency that allowed the inclusion of eleven personal and highly insightful interviews. These conversations took the book to another level. Thank you for your friendship and the example of your leadership.

Joey Paul with Thomas Nelson, it's rare to find a group so collaborative in spirit and gifted in skill. Thank you, Joey, for patiently answering my questions and bringing wisdom to the table. Thank you, **Janene MacIvor**, for your dedication to quality and bringing such ease and excellence to the editing process and **Mark Glesne**, for your commitment to your authors and creativity in marketing.

Richie Hughes, my agent, for always being helpful and a great leader with a servant's heart. I'm so glad you know this business better than I do. Let's hit P. F. Chang's and see what else we can dream up!

Greg Ligon, for patiently pursuing getting a book from me for a couple of years and for our partnership through Leadership Network, a great group that serves thousands of leaders so very well.

Lesley Lewis, my executive assistant of ten years, for being the best "air-traffic controller" I know. Thank you for keeping it all moving forward with grace, poise, and a cheerful heart.

Peer Jambor, for stopping by my office and randomly asking how the book was coming along. When I told you things were great, but I still needed a good subtitle, you came up with one in less than five minutes that everyone loved. Stop by more often.

Matthew Pless and **Susan Meek**, for praying relentlessly for well over a year that I'd finish this book!

Patti Reiland, I love you and hope you can listen to my passion, including a gazillion more "What do you think about this sentence?" questions, for many more books to come!

NOTES

Part 1: Deep Foundational Decisions

1. Wikipedia, s.v. "Chick-Fil-A," last modified June 10, 2019, https://en .wikipedia.org/wiki/Chick-fil-A.
2. https://www.chick-fil-a.com/about/histroy.
3. Dee Ann Turner, *It's My Pleasure: The Impact of Extraordinary Talent and a Compelling Culture* (Boise, ID: Elevate Publishing, 2015), 15, 19.
4. Turner, *It's My Pleasure*, 15.
5. Turner, *It's My Pleasure*.
6. Turner, *It's My Pleasure*, 12.
7. Wikipedia, s.v. "Chick-Fil-A."

Chapter 1: Ownership

1. Flavius Josephus, *Josephus: The Essential Writings*, trans. Paul L. Maier (Grand Rapids, MI: Kregel Publications, 1988), 48–50.

Chapter 2: Belief

1. Ashley Evans, *No More Fear: Break the Power of Intimidation in 40 Days* (Springfield, MO: Influence Resources, 2012), 29.
2. Evans, *No More Fear*, 50.

Chapter 3: Identity

1. Wikipedia, s.v. "American Idol," last modified June 10, 2019, https://en .widipedia.org/wiki/American_Idol.
2. *American Idol*, https://abc.go.com/shows/american-idol.

3. Michael E. Frisina, *Influential Leadership: Change Your Behavior, Change Your Organization, Change Health Care* (Chicago, IL: Health Administration Press, 2011), 17.

4. Tasha Eurich, "What Self-Awareness Really Is: And How to Cultivate It," *Harvard Business Review*, January 4, 2018, https://hbr.org/2018/01/what -self-awareness-really-is-and-how-to-cultivate-it.

5. Terry Linhart, *The Self-Aware Leader: Discovering Your Blind Spots to Reach Your Ministry Potential* (Downers Grove, IL: InterVarsity Press, 2017), 29.

Chapter 4: Attentiveness

1. Kadi Cole, interview with Dan Reiland, Dacula, GA, February 25, 2019.

2. Cole, interview with Dan Reiland.

3. Cole, interview with Dan Reiland.

Chapter 5: Soul

1. Sam Chand, interview with Dan Reiland, Dacula, GA, January 7, 2019.

2. Chand, interview with Dan Reiland.

Part 2: Deliberate Character Development

1. Jeffrey L. Sheler, *TIME Commemorative Edition, Billy Graham, America's Preacher* (New York, NY: Time Books, 2018), 48.

2. Russ Busby, *Billy Graham, God's Ambassador* (Alexandria, VA: Time Books, Custom Publishing, 1999), 31.

3. Busby, *Billy Graham, God's Ambassador*, 32.

4. Busby, *Billy Graham, God's Ambassador*, 34.

5. Wikipedia, s.v. "List of Billy Graham's Crusades," last modified March 13, 2019, http://en.wikipedia.org/wiki/list_of_billy_graham_crusades.

6. Billy Graham, *Just As I Am: The Autobiography of Billy Graham* (New York, NY: HarperCollins, 1997), 128–29.

Chapter 7: Authority

1. Dan Reiland, *Amplified Leadership: 5 Practices to Establish Influence, Build People, and Impact Others for a Lifetime* (Lake Mary, FL: Charisma House, 2011), 189.

2. Jo Anne Lyon, interview with Dan Reiland, Lawrenceville, GA, January 16, 2019.

3. Lyon, interview with Dan Reiland.

4. Clay Scroggins, *How to Lead When You're Not in Charge: Leveraging Influence When You Lack Authority* (Grand Rapids, MI: Zondervan, 2017), 21.

5. Reiland, *Amplified Leadership*, 190.
6. Scriptures related to the transference of authority: Mark 1:21–28: Recognition of Jesus' authority; Mark 11:27–33: Recognition of Jesus' authority; John 5:26–27: Jesus' authority from the Father; John 10:17–18: Jesus' authority from the Father; John 17:1–2: Jesus' authority from the Father; John 19:11: Jesus' authority from the Father; Ephesians 1:18–23: Jesus' authority from the Father; Matthew 9:6–8: Jesus' authority from the Father; Luke 10:19: Jesus' authority to the disciples; Mark 3:14–15: Jesus' authority to the disciples; Matthew 28:18–20: Jesus' authority from the Father given to all believers.

Chapter 8: Adaptability

1. IRIS, "Comparison of the Size of Israel vs. New Jersey," *Information Regarding Israel's Security*, 2019, https://iris.org.il/sizemaps/new_jersey.php.

Chapter 9: Improvement

1. Wikipedia, s.v. "Stephen Curry," last modified June 11, 2019, https://en .wikipedia.org/wiki/Stephen_Curry.
2. American Montessori Society, "NBA Sensation Steph Curry Says Montessori Education a Key to His Success," *Cision PR Newswire*, October 13, 2013, https://www.prnewswire.com/news-releases/nba-sensation-stephen-curry -says-montessori-education-a-key-to-his-success-229710251.html.
3. Scott Davis, "How Stephen Curry Became the Best Shooter in the NBA," *Business Insider*, June 4, 2015, https://www.businessinsider.com/how-stephen -curry-became-best-shooter-in-the-nba-2015-6.
4. David Fleming, "Stephen Curry: The Full Circle: The Untold Stoy of How a Single Rickety Hoop in Rural Virginia Produced Two Generations of NBA Great, Including the Future-Shaping Golden Boy," ESPN, April 23, 2015, http://www.espn.com/espn/feature/story/_/id/12728744/how-golden-state -warriors-stephen-curry-became-nba-best-point-guard.
5. David Fleming, "Sports' Perfect 0.4 Seconds," ESPN, April 1, 2014, http:// www.espn.com/nba/story/_/id/10703246/golden-state-warriors-stephen -curry-reinventing-shooting-espn-magazine.
6. E-60 Profile, "Steph Curry's Unprecedented Journey to the NBA," ESPN, June 2, 2016, http://www.espn.com/video/clip?id=15908162.
7. Jerry Barca, "NBA MVP Stephen Curry Seizes the Moment and Delivers His Message," *Forbes*, May 8, 2015, https://www.forbes.com/sites/jerrybarca /2015/05/08/nba-mvp-stephen-curry-seizes-the-moment-and-delivers-his -message/#174d03676e1d.

8. Wikipedia, s.v. "Stephen Curry."

9. Mark Stein, "Stephen Curry Wins MVP for Second Straight Season," ESPN, May 10, 2016, http://www.espn.com/nba/story/_/id/15499690 /stephen-curry-golden-state-warriors-first-unanimous-most-valuable-player.

10. David Drury, interview with Dan Reiland, Lawrenceville, GA, February 8, 2019.

11. Drury, interview with Dan Reiland.

12. Drury, interview with Dan Reiland.

Chapter 10: Resilience

1. Carey Nieuwhof, interview with Dan Reiland, Dacula, GA, February 25, 2019.

2. Nieuwhof, interview with Dan Reiland.

3. Nieuwhof, interview with Dan Reiland.

4. Nieuwhof, interview with Dan Reiland.

5. Richard A. Swenson, *Margin: Restoring Emotional, Physical, Financial, and Time Reserves to Overloaded Lives* (Colorado Springs, CO: NavPress, 2005), 69.

Part 3: Daily Practical Disciplines

1. John C. Maxwell, interview with Dan Reiland, Dacula, GA, March 25, 2019.

2. Maxwell, interview with Dan Reiland.

3. Maxwell, interview with Dan Reiland.

4. Maxwell, interview with Dan Reiland.

5. Maxwell, interview with Dan Reiland.

6. Maxwell, interview with Dan Reiland.

Chapter 11: Direction

1. John Meakin, "Titanic Arrogance," *Vision*, Spring 2002, https://www.vision .org/titanic-arrogance-676.

2. Harold J. Sala, "Overconfidence," *Guidelines International*, February 22, 2016, https://www.guidelines.org/devotional/overconfidence/.

3. Pedro C. Ribeiro, "Sinking the Unsinkable: Lessons for Leadership," *Nasa / Appel Knowledge Services*, August 2, 2012, https://appel.nasa.gov/2012/08/02 /sinking-the-unsinkable-lessons-for-leadership/.

4. History.com, "Titanic," *A&E Networks / Global Media and Entertainment Brand Portfolio*, Original published November 9, 2009; updated August 21, 2019, https://www.history.com/topics/early-20th-century-us/titanic.

5. Peter Corning, "Lessons of the Titanic: A Tragic Tale of Hubris and Human Errors, and a Litany of 'What Ifs,'" *Psychology Today*, April 12, 2012, https://www.psychologytoday.com/us/blog/the-fair-society/201204/lessons-the -titanic.

6. Meakin, "Titanic Arrogance."

7. Carey Nieuwhof, host, Episode 206: "Les McKeown on Visionaries, Operators and Processors and How Each is Necessary in Thriving Operations," Carey Nieuwhof Leadership Podcast (MP3 podcast), August 7, 2018, https://careynieuwhof.com/episode206/.

8. Wikipedia, s.v. "Project Management Triangle," last modified May 23, 2019, http://en.wikipedia.org/wiki/project_management_triangle.

9. Jenni Catron, interview with Dan Reiland, Dacula, GA, March 11, 2019.

10. Catron, interview with Dan Reiland.

11. Catron, interview with Dan Reiland.

Chapter 12: Focus

1. Al Ries, *Focus: The Future of Your Company Depends on It* (New York, NY: Harper Business, 1996), Introduction.

2. Ries, *Focus*, 2–3.

3. Chris Hodges, interview with Dan Reiland, Dacula, GA, March 20, 2019.

4. Hodges, interview with Dan Reiland.

5. Hodges, interview with Dan Reiland.

6. Hodges, interview with Dan Reiland.

7. Hodges, interview with Dan Reiland.

8. Hodges, interview with Dan Reiland.

9. Good Reads, s.v. "Confucius Quotes," https://goodreads.com/quotes /8688305.

Chapter 13: Heart

1. Crawford Loritts, interview with Dan Reiland, Dacula, GA, May 6, 2019.

2. Loritts, interview with Dan Reiland.

3. Loritts, interview with Dan Reiland.

4. Loritts, interview with Dan Reiland.

5. Loritts, interview with Dan Reiland.

6. Loritts, interview with Dan Reiland.

7. Loritts, interview with Dan Reiland.

8. Loritts, interview with Dan Reiland.

9. Loritts, interview with Dan Reiland.

Chapter 14: Communication

1. Ashley Wooldridge, interview with Dan Reiland, Dacula, GA, May 22, 2019.
2. Wooldridge, interview with Dan Reiland.
3. Wooldridge, interview with Dan Reiland.
4. Wooldridge, interview with Dan Reiland.
5. Wooldridge, interview with Dan Reiland.
6. Wooldridge, interview with Dan Reiland.

Chapter 15: Mentoring

1. Joshua's Men program, founded in 1987, by Dan Reiland, is in thousands of churches as an intensive leadership development program. The entire curriculum is free of charge as part of the church resources made available through 12Stone Church. You can find it here: https://resources.12stone.com.
2. Jerry Hurley, interview with Dan Reiland, Dacula, GA, May 2, 2019.
3. Hurley, interview with Dan Reiland.
4. Hurley, interview with Dan Reiland.
5. Hurley, interview with Dan Reiland.
6. Craig Groeschel is the senior pastor of Life Church.
7. Hurley, interview with Dan Reiland.
8. Hurley, interview with Dan Reiland.

BIBLIOGRAPHY

American Idol, ABC, https://abc.go.com/shows/american-idol.

American Montessori Society, "NBA Sensation Steph Curry Says Montessori Education a Key to His Success." *Cision PR Newswire*. October 13, 2013. https://www.prnewswire.com/news-releases/nba-sensation-stephen-curry -says-montessori-education-a-key-to-his-success-229710251.html.

Barca, Jerry. "NBA MVP Stephen Curry Seizes the Moment and Delivers His Message." *Forbes*. May 8, 2015. https://www.forbes.com/sites/jerrybarca /2015/05/08/nba-mvp-stephen-curry-seizes-the-moment-and-delivers-his -message/#174d03676e1d.

Brown, Brené. *Dare to Lead: Brave Work. Tough Conversations. Whole Hearts.* New York, NY: Random House, 2018.

Busby, Russ. *Billy Graham, God's Ambassador.* Alexandria, VA: Time Books, Custom Publishing, 1999.

Corning, Peter. "Lessons of the Titanic: A Tragic Tale of Hubris and Human Errors, and a Litany of 'What Ifs." *Psychology Today*. April 12, 2012. https:// www.psychologytoday.com/us/blog/the-fair-society/201204/lessons-the -titanic.

Davis, Scott. "How Steph Curry Became the Best Shooter in the NBA." *Business Insider*. June 4, 2015. https://www.businessinsider.com/how-stephen-curry -became-best-shooter-in-the-nba-2015-6.

E-60 Profile. "Steph Curry's Unprecedented Journey to the NBA." ESPN. June 2, 2016. http://www.espn.com/video/clip?id=15908162.

Eurich, Tasha. "What Self-Awareness Really Is: And How to Cultivate It." *Harvard Business Review*. January 4, 2018. https://hbr.org/2018/01/what-self -awareness-really-is-and-how-to-cultivate-it.

Evans, Ashely. *No More Fear: Break the Power of Intimidation in 40 Days.* Springfield, MO: Influence Resources, 2012.

Fleming, David. "Full Circle: The Untold Story of How a Single Rickety Hoop in Rural Virginia Produced Two Generations of NBA Great, Including the Future-Shaping Golden Boy." ESPN. April 23, 2015. http://www.espn.com /espn/feature/story/_/id/12728744/how-golden-state-warriors-stephen-curry -became-nba-best-point-guard.

----------. "Sports' Perfect 0.4 Seconds." ESPN. April 1, 2014. http://www.espn .com/nba/story/_/id/10703246/golden-state-warriors-stephen-curry -reinventing-shooting-espn-magazine.

Frisina, Michael E. *Influential Leadership: Change Your Behavior, Change Your Organization, Change Health Care.* Chicago, IL: Health Administration Press, 2011.

Goleman, Daniel, Richard Boyatzis, and Annie McKee. *Primal Leadership: Unleashing the Power of Emotional Intelligence.* Boston, MA: Harvard Business Review Press, 2013.

Good Reads, s.v. "Confucius Quotes," https://goodreads.com/quotes/8688305.

Graham, Billy. *Just As I Am: The Autobiography of Billy Graham.* New York, NY: HarperCollins, 1997.

History.com. "Titanic," *A&E Networks / Global Media and Entertainment Brand Portfolio.* Original published November 9, 2009; last modified June 9, 2010. https://www.history.com/topics/early-20th-century-us/titanic.

IRIS. "Comparison of the Size of Israel vs. New Jersey." *Information Regarding Israel's Security.* 2019. https://iris.org.il/sizemaps/new_jersey.php.

Josephus, Flavius. *Josephus: The Essential Writings.* Translated by Maier, Paul L. Grand Rapids, MI: Kregel Publications, 1988.

Linhart, Terry. *The Self-Aware Leader: Discovering Your Blind Spots to Reach Your Ministry Potential.* Downers Grove, IL: InterVarsity Press, 2017.

Meakin, John. "Titanic Arrogance." *Vision.* Spring 2002. https://www.vision.org /titanic-arrogance-676.

Nieuwhof, Cary, host. Episode 206: "Les McKcKeown on Visionaries, Operators and Processors and How Each is Necessary in Thriving Operations." Carey Nieuwhof Leadership Podcast (MP3 podcast). Posted on August 7, 2018. https://careynieuwhof.com/episode206/.

Reiland, Dan. *Amplified Leadership: 5 Practices to Establish Influence, Build People and Impact Others for a Lifetime.* Lake Mary, FL: Charisma House, 2011.

Reis, Al. *Focus: The Future of Your Company Depends on It.* New York, NY: Harper Business, 1996.

Ribeiro, Pedro C. "Sinking the Unthinkable: Lessons for Leadership." Nasa / Appel Knowledge Services. August 2, 2012. https://appel.nasa.gov/2012/08 /02/sinking-the-unsinkable-lessons-for-leadership/.

Sala, Harold J. "Overconfidence." *Guidelines International*. February 22, 2016. https://www.guidelines.org/devotional/overconfidence/.

Scroggins, Clay. *How to Lead When You're Not in Charge: Leveraging Influence When You Lack Authority*. Grand Rapids, MI: Zondervan, 2017.

Sheler, Jeffrey L. *TIME Commemorative Edition, Billy Graham, America's Preacher*. New York, NY: Time Books, 2018.

Stein, Mark. "Stephen Curry Wins MVP for Second Straight Season." ESPN. May 11, 2016. http://www.espn.com/nba/story/_/id/15499690/stephen -curry-golden-state-warriors-first-unanimous-most-valuable-player.

Swenson, Richard A. *Margin: Restoring Emotional, Physical, Financial, and Time Resources to Overloaded Lives*. Colorado Springs, CO: NavPress, 2005.

Tozer, A.W. *The Pursuit of God*. CreateSpace.com: CreateSpace Independent Publishing Platform, 2019.

Turner, Dee Ann. *It's My Pleasure: The Impact of Extraordinary Talent and a Compelling Culture*. Boise, ID: Elevate Publishing, 2015.

ABOUT THE AUTHOR

Dan Reiland has been a pastor and leader for thirty-nine years. He served alongside John C. Maxwell for twenty years, first as executive pastor at Skyline Church, then as VP of Leadership and Church Development for Injoy Ministries. Dan is the author of four books, including leadership titles *Shoulder to Shoulder* and *Amplified Leadership*. He blogs regularly and is considered among the top church consultants and leadership coaches. For the past nineteen years, Dan has served as executive pastor of 12Stone Church in Lawrenceville, Georgia. He and his wife, Patti, have two children.